No More Excuses

You Are Destined For Greatness

Terra Dobson

Copyright © 2019 by Terra Dobson

All rights reserved. No part of this publication may be reproduced by any means, graphics, electronic, or mechanical, including photocopying, recording, taping, or by any information storage retrieval system without the written permission of the publisher except in the case of brief quotations embodied in critical articles and reviews.

Terra Dobson/Rejoice Essential Publishing
PO BOX 512
Effingham, SC 29541

www.republishing.org

Unless otherwise indicated, scripture is taken from the King James Version.

Scripture quotations marked (NLT) are taken from the Holy Bible, New Living Translation, copyright ©1996, 2004, 2015 by Tyndale House Foundation. Used by permission of Tyndale House Publishers, a Division of Tyndale House Ministries, Carol Stream, Illinois 60188. All rights reserved.

Scripture quotations marked (NIV) are taken from the Holy Bible, New International Version®, NIV®. Copyright © 1973, 1978, 1984, 2011 by Biblica, Inc.™ Used by permission of Zondervan. All rights reserved worldwide. www.zondervan.com The "NIV" and "New International Version" are trademarks registered in the United States Patent and Trademark Office by Biblica, Inc.™

Scripture quotations marked (ESV) are taken from The Holy Bible, English Standard Version® (ESV®) Copyright © 2001 by Crossway, a publishing ministry of Good News Publishers. All rights reserved.

The Holy Bible, Berean Study Bible, BSB Copyright ©2016, 2018 by Bible Hub. Used by Permission. All Rights Reserved Worldwide.

Scripture taken from the New King James Version®. Copyright © 1982 by Thomas Nelson. Used by permission. All rights reserved..

No More Excuses/ Terra Dobson

ISBN-13: 978-1-952312-35-9

Library of Congress Control Number: 2020919286

Dedication

To My Heavenly Father, thank you for your unconditional love and always pushing me to go Higher in you.

To my mom, Linda Searcy, who has always been there for me and has always been my greatest supporter.

To my Dad, in loving memory of, Gary Dobson, whom I learned to trust God beyond impossibilities.

To my siblings, Tina (your husband Kelvin), Erika (your husband Michael), and Ian (your wife Erika). You guys are the best siblings ever. I appreciate your endless support.

To my nieces and nephew, I love you all.

To my grandmother, Virginia Stroud, thank you for being an inspiration and a source of strength.

To my great uncle, William Majors aka Uncle Bill, your humor and support means more than you'll ever know.

To my cousin, Torin Dobson, I want to give you a special thank you for the photography.

To my entire family (living and those who have gone to be with the Lord), thank you for always supporting and encouraging me. I love you all.

The reader, I hope this book will inspire you to SOAR!

Contents

ACKNOWLEDGMENTS..................................xi

FOREWORD...xii

CHAPTER 1: Stop Procrastination........1

CHAPTER 2: No More Excuses............17

CHAPTER 3: The Power of Connection....................34

CHAPTER 4: Overcoming Fear & Knowing Who You Are In Christ..................56

CHAPTER 5: Take God at His Word................................75

ABOUT THE AUTHOR...................................98

Acknowledgments

I want to give a heartfelt thank you to Prophetess Kimberly Moses. Thank you for giving me the push I needed to write and complete this book. My mentors, friends, my current Pastor, Dr. Damond E. Bragg, and those leaders (Pastors) who helped shape my character and always encouraged me to keep moving forward in my purpose. I want to give a huge shout out to Bishop Umiko D. Jones, Sr. for writing the foreword.

Foreword

As a pastor, it is not often that I come across an individual who is committed to carrying out their purpose with sincere intentionality. An individual that recognizes their struggles and does the difficult work to honestly and diligently to overcome them. People like that are rare jewels and they are unforgettable. I met Terra when she was being ordained into ministry several years ago. She exuded a quiet and calm demeanor and yet the power of her conviction about the calling on her life was evident. It has been my privilege to witness from afar how Terra has developed and matured both personally and ministerially.

In these five chapters, Terra walks us through God's amazing transformation in her life as she acknowledged, accepted, and applied His Word in her life. She speaks with a refreshing level of transparency, which helps the reader to picture themselves and respond to the many questions and struggles addressed in each chapter.

Each chapter encourages us to push through the enemy's lies and deceptive tactics to pursue our divine purpose by overcoming procrastination and fear. Also, to leave our excuses behind as we make Godly connections that help us to acknowledge who we are in Christ. In so doing, we will ultimately see the purposes of God manifest in our lives as we take hold of His Promises.

I believe everyone who reads this book will be blessed as they encounter and internalize the principles that are presented.

Umiko D. Jones Sr.
First Assistant Presiding Bishop
Victory United Fellowship of Churches

CHAPTER 1

Stop Procrastination

You might be saying to yourself, "I will put this off to do at a later day and time." Just know, tomorrow isn't promised to anyone. God placed you on this earth for such a time as this, which means you have a time frame to accomplish everything that God has placed within you. Decide to be brave! Declare with me: "I will no longer delay the ideas and the assignment God is asking me to do for His glory."

You might ask, "What is procrastination?" Wikipedia defines it as the avoidance of doing a task that needs to be accomplished by a certain deadline. Procrastination is one of the greatest tricks the enemy uses against you to keep you from fulfilling your God-given purpose. The enemy wants you to defer your destiny. Once more, I must reiterate this to you, God has given you a time frame to do His bidding within the earth. If the enemy can keep you preoccupied with the cares of life, or simply waiting and being idle, he can steal your destiny. The Scripture in John 10:10 states that the thief does not come except to steal, kill, and destroy. Jesus boldy declared, I have come that they may have life, and they may have it more abundantly. Procrastination will rob you of success. It will keep you stuck in dead end situations. God has given you the power to overcome procrastination. Be determined. Have a made up mind that you will no longer be stuck or put your life on hold.

Let's break John 10:10 down a little further. First, the enemy's ultimate goal is to assassinate and derail you from walking in your God-given purpose. You were created to be an effective representative of the Kingdom of God. No matter what lies the enemy might be speaking, you are fearfully and wonderfully made according to Psalms 139. You have value and possess purpose! One of Satan's biggest lies is to plant false ideas in your mind of who you were designed to be. To steal... the enemy wants you stuck in limbo and living your life in confusion. You don't have to question or doubt your identity.

As I write this book, one of the lies running in my mind is, "You'll never complete this book. You don't have what it takes to write this book. Just wait until tomorrow and you can start working on it then." I refuse to stop until this book is written. I am reminded of the Scripture in Philippians 4:13, "I can do all things through Christ who strengthens me."

In my personal life, I have wasted so much time running around trying to convince people of the things God wants to do in my life. While you're trying to find people to agree with you, guess what? You are procrastinating and simply wasting time. Only you know the things God has placed within your heart. Be confident! You are hearing from God clearly and you can walk boldly in the plans He is revealing to you. The Holy Spirit is your biggest cheerleader! John 16:13 says, "However, when He, the Spirit of truth, has come, He will guide you into all truth; for He will not speak on His own authority, but whatever He hears He will speak; and He will tell you things to come." Rely on the Holy Spirit. He will confirm the purpose God wants you to fulfill.

I want to encourage you to no longer be satisfied with the status quo. God hasn't called you to be stuck or continually putting your life on hold. There comes a time when you have to, "Just do it!" In other words, you have to step out in faith! You might not have all the answers. In Genesis 12:1, we read that God tells Abraham to leave His country. Abraham didn't have all the answers, but he knew he had to obey the call of God on his life. If Abraham would have procrastinated, then he would have missed the calling and timing of God. Abraham didn't have time to convince his family God had called him. If Abraham waited for his family's approval, he would have cheated himself out of the timing of God. If you spend time trying to convince people of what God is speaking to you, then it becomes a time robber. In my life, I had to learn that not everyone will understand and agree with the vision God has given to you. If you want to convince anyone, convince yourself. If God be for you, then who can be against you! There will come a time in your life when you will have to stand alone. Like Abraham, you might not have all the blueprint at one time. With a heart of bravery, be determined to keep moving and to trust God. As you refuse to stand still and stuck in limbo, God will give you directions when you're willing to go and obey, with each step you take.

We waste so much time seeking other's approval and validation that we miss the timing of God. When we seek approval from others, all it does is add confusion to our minds. If we don't get the answer we need, it causes us to become immobile. We stop doing what God has spoken to us. Hence, we sit in limbo waiting for someone to come along to confirm what we should be doing. All it does is adds confusion and we take one more trip around the dreaded mountain of procrastination. For example, if you buy a MacBook

Air from the Apple Store, you wouldn't call the helpline at Hewlett Packard to understand your product. No, you would call the customer service line at Apple. Likewise, for a believer, in Christ, we need to stay in prayer with the Holy Spirit to confirm the blueprint God has given to us. John 14:26 says, "But the Helper, the Holy Spirit, whom the Father will send in My name, He will teach you all things, and bring to your remembrance all that I said to you." Another one of my favorite Scriptures comes to mind, Proverbs 3:5-6, "Trust in the LORD with all your heart and lean not on your own understanding; in all your ways submit to him, and he will make your paths straight. God has equipped us with the tools we need to defeat and overcome procrastination.

Procrastination is a mere time stealer. It robs one from fulfilling the things God wants to do in your life. Stop waiting on people to agree with you. Another false perception is we think everything in our lives has to be perfect in order to walk in God's plan. Just stop it! Things will never be perfect. You'll always hope to have more money in the bank, more time, or perhaps, living in a bigger/better house. Or whatever the lie is, you keep telling yourself you need to be just right before you do God's will. Sadly, it may never happen at one time or might not happen at all. You have to move now!!! There is an urgency to move now! Why? Time waits on no one! John 9:4 (NLT) says, "We must quickly carry out the tasks assigned us by the one who sent us. The night is coming, and then no one can work." There is an urgency in the heavenly realm for you to walk in the assignment God has given to you. Don't allow false expectations to cause you to miss God's timing.

You have to trust and believe as you begin to walk in purpose, God will take care of everything concerning you. If you want your life to change for the better, then be willing to put the work in. Be prepared to move when God says move. It comes down to the choices we make. Your choices have to line up with the expectations or the direction you want your life to go. Be determined, no matter what. I want the best God has for me. Be willing to make changes that will produce results for God's best! God hasn't called you to live a life of mediocrity. He wants you to live your best life!

Refuse to wish your life away! God wants us to live a life guided by faith. You can have faith to believe things will change for the better; unfortunately, if your faith isn't fueled by action, you will still be stuck. As the Scripture states, faith without works is dead. You will take one more trip down the road of procrastination, which will cause you to be hopeless. Instead of running toward the promises of God, you will be dragging your feet toward His promises. God hasn't given us a spirit of procrastination. He's given you a spirit of you can do all things through Christ, who provides strength for you. Repeat after me, "I CAN DO IT!" Declare with me, "I will no longer be stuck in a dead situation and not put forth an effort to get out of it." You were created to shine. You weren't designed to sit on the sideline. God has given you a performance on the main stage. It's your time! It's time for you to shine in the spotlight of God's glory!

It's time to take your rightful place in the body of Christ. I hear the cliché coming to mind, "I'm waiting on God." Listen here people of God. We've got to stop using this as a crutch. The reality is we are the ones out of alignment. God is waiting on us to obey Him. God wants us to get in motion with His instructions and to move accordingly. It reminds me of the Scripture in the Bible when Jesus approached the man who was lying at the pool. In this Scripture, an angel came down into the pool to trouble the water. Jesus, simply asked the man, do you want to be made whole (John 5:1-15)? We have to ask ourselves the same. Do I want victory in my life? Am I willing to be made whole? Have the determination to do whatever it takes to become victorious. Receive the freedom God has given to you and position yourself to accomplish God's plans for you!

God gives us twenty-four hours in a day to accomplish His will. It's up to us to decide what we are going to do with our time. God isn't going to force us to use our time wisely. It's up to us to map our day and to make effective use of our time. You have to choose to maximize your potential for each given day. The first step to breaking the spirit of procrastination is to ask yourself, "Am I willing to put the work in?" In other words, how bad do you want the blessings of the LORD to be displayed in your life? Be willing to work! Proverbs 6:6-9 says, "Go to the ant, you sluggard!

Consider her ways and be wise, which, having no captain, overseer or ruler, provides her supplies in the summer, and gathers her food in the harvest. How long will you slumber, O sluggard? When will you rise from your sleep?" Be willing to roll up your sleeves to do the work. The work might include finding Scriptures to memorize regarding procrastination. Another step might be hiring a life coach. More importantly, we have the help of the Holy Spirit. If need be, fast and pray to ask God to help you to break the spirit of procrastination.

Secondly, you have to set goals for each day. If that means creating a list of things to achieve within a given day, then do so. Purchase a calendar that has a weekly breakout. Plan your week accordingly. Stick with the plan you have mapped out for each week. Be consistent and don't waiver from the goals you established. Stay focused! Too often, we get distracted by doing stuff God hasn't ordained us to do. Instead of pleasing God, we try to please people. Not everyone is going to be happy with the choices you make. That's perfectly okay as long as your choices are pleasing and bringing honor to God. The point is don't allow people to manipulate you from God's will for your life. Don't be afraid to tell people no and that isn't God's will for you. It's okay to say no! Try it with me, "NO!" It's okay to use it as a complete sentence without any explanation. Don't be afraid to use the word, no. Proverbs 29:25 (NLT) says, "Fearing people is a dangerous trap, but trusting the LORD means safety."

Thirdly, you must find some people who will be your accountability partners. People who will hold you accountable to staying on or sticking with the task. Pray to God to give you the right people who will encourage you when you feel like giving up, or throwing in the towel. At this second, God wanted me to encourage you with this, "Don't quit!" Galatians 6:9 says, "Let us not become weary in doing good, for at the proper time we will reap a harvest if we do not give up." Did you hear that? If you stay focused and consistent, there is a reward coming to you! Your accountability partners should be people who want to see you succeed. These people will encourage you, pray for you, and assist you with the vision God has given to you.

For example, when you go to the gym, most people have a personal trainer to help them stay on track to make sure they are doing and completing their exercises properly. Likewise, we shouldn't feel ashamed to ask for help from likeminded people. God sent people will be more than happy to assist you in your areas of weakness. Please ask God to illuminate these people to you! Ask God to give you wisdom to choose these people. Ask God for discernment to be able to distinguish who is sent by Him. You can identify these people if they have an authentic relationship with God and if these people display Godly characteristics. Matthew 7:16 states, "Ye shall know them by their fruits. Do men gather grapes of thorns, or figs of thistles?"

Be aware of those people who smile in your face and say the right words, but when you're not present, it is a different story. God will clearly show you who's who. With the Holy Spirit's help, you quickly learn not everyone has your best interest at heart. When you prayerfully seek God, He will assign people to assist you in your journey.

In the body of Christ, we must be willing to help each other. According to Romans 15:1, the stronger members must bear the infirmities of the weaker ones. When I say weaker ones, what I mean is, we are all on different stages of growth in our walk with the Lord. No one in the body of Christ has the right to be looking down at another member. I don't care how long you've been walking with God. No one has the right to have the 'I'm better than you' mentality. It's only by God's grace that we grow and obtain a deeper revelation of God's truth. If we see another member who isn't at the level we're at then let's motivate them to come up higher in God. Don't gossip about your brother or sister in Christ or talk about them. Simply, pray for them, speak God's truth to them in love, and encourage them to do good works. The same attitude should be applied if we see our brothers/sisters in Christ overtaken by sin. 1 Corinthians 12:26 says, "If one part suffers, every part suffers with it. If one part is honored, every part rejoices with it." In essence, we are our brother and sister keepers. In the body of Christ, we need each other to survive and thrive. God wants us to have authentic love towards one another. God's love covers and it protects! "Above all, love each other deeply, because love covers a multitude of sins." (1 Peter 4:8).

I never want to leave the impression that it's okay to willfully sin. It's not okay! Sin blocks your purpose and your relationship with God. If you are struggling with sin in any area of your life, cry out to God, He will help you with that bad habit or addiction. God is faithful and just to cleanse you from all unrighteousness. Lastly, if you need help to overcome sin or if you are struggling with anything in your life, don't be afraid to reach out to your accountability partner for help.

As an accountability partner, you have to drop jealousy and pride. We must stop being judgmental and critical towards one another. We are called to love each other. If we see someone falling behind, drop your negativity towards that person and help them to get back in the race. We are called the body because we need one another to win this race called life. Make sure you help your person stay on track. Instead of hailing a committee meeting about a person doing a task ineffectively, build them up with words of encouragement. We are all running a race. It doesn't matter how fast you start out. Your objective is to make it to the finish line. Therefore, refuse to allow procrastination to cause you to be an ineffective runner in the race. God hasn't called any of His children to sit on the side-line to be idle and watch things happen. No, He wants all of His children to be effective for His kingdom. It's time for you to shake off the setbacks, delays, and denials. I hear the Father saying, "It's time for you to get in the runner's position! On your mark, get set, go!" Go be great! Destiny is beckoning you to step into greatness!

My Testimony

I never would've thought I would be writing a book. If you're reading this book, just know I overcame procrastination. If I can do it, you can too!!! There is nothing extraordinary about me, except the fact that I believed God and stepped out on the wings of faith! I know with God all things are possible and I was willing to do the work to write a book. One more side note...Never let anyone tell you don't have what it takes in order to be successful. You have the DNA of the Father on the inside of you, which means you, my brother/sister in Christ, you're a winner. You are more than victorious through Christ. YOU GOT THIS! Declare with me, "With God on my side, I won't be stopped!"

Prayer

LORD, help me to no longer be stagnated and waste time. Help me to rely on your Holy Spirit to overcome procrastination. Help me to use my time wisely. Help me to maximize my potential for each day You give me. In Jesus' Name, Amen.

CHAPTER 2

No More Excuses

We use so many excuses as to why we can't do something. An excuse can be anything from I don't have time, I don't have what it takes, I don't have enough money, or I'm not smart enough. You don't have to rely on yourself to fulfill God's purpose for you. God never called us to accomplish anything in our strength and power. He empowers us through His Holy Spirit to get the job done. I hear the Spirit of God saying, "It's time to drop the excuses. It's time for you to arise. Your voice needs to be heard within the earth." Just know you are capable of doing the assignment God has given to you.

You might ask, "What is an excuse?" An excuse, as defined by the Collins dictionary, is a reason that you give to explain why something has been done or has not been done, or in order to avoid doing something. My friend, you have just been served. The time for excuses is over. As I mentioned, in the previous chapter, how bad do you want to be all the Creator of the universe has ordained you to become? At the beginning of 2019, the word the LORD gave me was, NO MORE EXCUSES! Ouch! That really stepped on my toes. What a revelation to me! It wasn't what I wanted to hear, but what I needed to hear to move into the next phase of my destiny. I invite you to join this journey with me. What excuses are you using that's hindering you from fulfilling your purpose and living your best life?

It's time for us to stop putting off the things God has placed within our hearts. Join this brave fight with me and declare, "I will no longer live under the umbrella of excuses!" It's time for me to walk in purpose! I will no longer continue running on the hamster's wheel of excuses. It's time to break every stronghold that's hindering you from being your best you. Drop the spiritual crutches and walk victoriously towards your 'Promised Land'.

We will examine people in the Bible who had tons of excuses, but God wasn't willing to allow them to use those things to keep them side-lined from their purpose. Isn't it funny how we try to tell Elohim, God, our Creator, the things we aren't capable of doing? It's funny because He is the Creator of the universe. This is the same Creator, we read about in Genesis 1:1-10, who created the heavens and the earth. This is the same God who spoke the world into existence. We forget how powerful He is. The same God, who in Jeremiah 32:27, declared, "Behold, I am the LORD, the God of all flesh, is there anything too hard for me?" Therefore, God knows what He's placed inside of us and yet we tell Him we're not qualified. The bottom line is you are capable.

In the Old Testament, we see the people who were called by God gave a plethora of excuses as to why they couldn't be used to carry out their God-given assignments. Often, we're critical of them, but we do the same thing today. We use every excuse in the book as to why we can't obey the call of God. Let's examine some of the excuses. If you fall into one of these categories, repent! Ask the Father to strengthen you in these areas. We will discuss later the ministry calls of Jeremiah and Moses. I love the Scripture in Zechariah 4:6 (NIV), "Not by might nor by power, but by my Spirit, 'says the LORD Almighty." God is saying, "You don't have to do it in your own strength. It's my Spirit that does the work." All God needs us to do is to say yes to His leading and His promptings.

Luke 10:2 says, "The harvest is plentiful, but the workers are few." Did you hear that? God needs you! You were uniquely made! He needs your help to reach the lost; those who don't know Him or have a personal relationship with HIM. There are people waiting to hear your testimony, waiting on you to pray for them, encourage them, and simply needing to see a demonstration of God's love. Don't allow excuses to keep you from being an effective witness of God's power and love. No one can be you and express the things God has done for you. You're a designer original. No one can duplicate your personality or the ministry God has given to you. You are God's masterpiece. No one can be you, except you! This should eliminate some of the pressure you might feel from thoughts of being inadequate or always thinking you don't fit in. Guess what? You don't fit in! Simply, because you were created to be one of a kind. Now, take a deep breath! I hope this has sunk in that you don't have to be like everyone else. You don't have to compete with anyone. You are enough! You have unique gifts that God has placed within you. It might be a shock to us. However, who we are and the gifting we carry isn't a shock to God. God knew you when you were in your mother's womb according to Jeremiah 1. God has equipped and empowered us with everything we need to be successful.

Excuses are false perceptions that we allow to keep us in a life of mediocrity. When God gives us a vision, our first thought is, "LORD, I can't do this." We focus on our limitations instead of focusing on God, who can do all things. This wrong thinking is a form of idolatry. Repent! Take your focus off you and place your eyes on Jesus! Just know if God has given you an assignment, then He's given you everything you need to accomplish the task. Make this declaration with me, "I can do all things through Christ, who empowers me." Drop the 'what if I fail,' 'what if I'm not capable!' There will always be the "what if's" in life. However, we've got to change our mindset and replace those negative thoughts with faith.

Hebrews 11:6 says, "But without faith it is impossible to please God, for he that cometh to God must believe that he is, and that he is a rewarder of those that diligently seek Him." Instead of the dreaded 'what if's,' let's try, "This might be the best thing that ever happened to me. I got this because He has me. I may not be able to do it in my own strength, but with the Spirit of the living God dwelling on the inside me, I can do this!" YOU were not created to live a mediocre life. YOU were not created to be the underdog. YOU were not ordained to live a life of fear and the decisions you make to be controlled by fear.

We quote this Scripture quite often in our churches. The Scripture is 2 Timothy 1:7, "For God has not given us a SPIRIT OF FEAR, but of POWER and of Love and of a SOUND MIND." We've got to do more than just quote this Scripture! However, the question remains, do you believe it? Do you? You have to know beyond a shadow of a doubt that you were created to be fearless!

As I mentioned earlier, let's look at some of the excuses used by those God called in the Old Testament. Let's not beat ourselves up too bad over some of the excuses we have given God. However, if you find yourself using some of these excuses, repent and ask the Father to help you see yourself the way He sees you. Also, ask HIM to help you rely on the assistance of the HOLY SPIRIT. In Jeremiah 1:6, the LORD called Jeremiah to be a prophet to the nations. A prophet is a person regarded as an inspired teacher or proclaimer of the will of God (Oxford dictionary). Jeremiah was seventeen when God called him into ministry. I'm sure Jeremiah thought, "LORD, these people won't listen to me. I'm not quite as old as they are." Jeremiah's response to

God was, "Then said I, Ah, Lord God! Behold, I cannot speak: for I am a child." God didn't care about Jeremiah's age.

The only thing God was concerned about was having a trust worthy vessel. This same viewpoint applies to us now. God doesn't care about what you think is an inadequacy. He just wants to know if you will say yes and keep your heart pure. Please never forget that God is the potter and we are the clay. We must remain teachable and humble before the LORD. As Jeremiah relied on the LORD to fill his mouth with divine inspiration, we must rely on God to do the same for us. I love what God said to Jeremiah. We see the Lord's response in Jeremiah 1:7, which says, "But the Lord said unto me, Say not, I am a child: for thou shalt go to all that I shall send thee, and whatsoever I command thee thou shalt speak." I'm grateful that God isn't a God who practices age discrimination. It doesn't matter how old you are. The reality is that God can USE you. The Father wants you to say yes to HIS leading and HIS promptings.

You might have gotten a late start in life. You might think you're too old to be used by God or you missed your window of opportunity! Be at peace. It's not too late for God to execute His plan for your life. Rest assured my friend! It's never too late. Allow me to let you in on this secret, if you're reading this book, and the mere fact that God allowed you to see another day, means He has a great work for you. He has a marvelous plan for your life and there's hope! I love the Scripture in Joel. It is about how God will restore the wasted years in your life. Joel 2:25 says, "And I will restore to you the years." God is a God of restoration. He wants to give you back everything you thought you lost. Or on the other hand, like Jeremiah, you might think you're too young. Whatever the case may be, you have what it takes to answer the call. Just rely on the Holy Spirit to lead and to teach you.

It's the Holy Spirit that's doing the work. Whew, that takes the pressure off of us trying to do God's work in our strength and power. We can rest in HIM knowing it's the Holy Spirit giving us the blueprint. God didn't allow Jeremiah to use the excuse of age. He later assured Jeremiah that He would be with him and that He would place His words in his mouth. Jeremiah 1:9 says, Then the LORD put forth His hand, and touched my mouth. And the LORD said unto me, Behold, I have put my words in thy mouth." The Holy Spirit will give you wisdom. He will give you the words to say. God wants you to answer the call and to not allow fear to paralyze you from moving forward in your purpose. The LORD told Joshua in Joshua 1:1, "Only be strong and courageous." You might feel fear, but you don't have to allow it to control you and stop you from walking into your purpose.

The next person we look at will be that of Moses. As you recall, when God called Moses, he was attending his father-in-law's sheep and goats. Moses heard a voice calling him out of a burning bush. When Moses gazed upon the bush, it wasn't consumed by the fire. Finally, the LORD had gotten Moses' attention. The call of Moses can be found in Exodus 3:1-10. Like Moses, God will only allow us to go so far away from our purpose. When the time is right and our hearts are ready to receive truth, God will reveal Himself to us in the same way He did to Moses. You might be running from God's plan for your life. The reality is one day you'll have to stop running and walking in rebellion against God. Ultimately, you can't run or hide from the purpose God has ordained for you. Cry out to God and ask Him to forgive you for being disobedient. As you surrender, God will forgive you and He will give you instructions as He did with Moses. In the example of Moses, God called him to be a deliverer for His chosen people Israel. God wanted him to deliver his people from the tyranny of the Egyptian Pharaoh. Now, that God has your attention, are you willing to adhere to the instructions? Are you ready to accept the assignment and to jump into your greatness whole-heartedly?

Let's examine the five excuses Moses tried to use with God. The first excuse Moses tried to give was, I am nobody (Exodus 3:11). Just like Moses, you might be thinking, "I am nobody. How can God use me?" I love how God uses ordinary people. Don't focus on your inadequacies and natural limitations. I advise you my friend to focus on the strength and power of God. For example, when it comes to myself, I have a quiet, shy and quirky personality. However, when I preach, I become bold and loud. The fear and timidity goes out the window! I realize it's not me doing the preaching; it's the Holy Spirit working through me. Sometimes, I get so nervous, I have to place page markers in my Bible to locate Scriptures, while I'm preaching and teaching. I can be a whole hot mess! However, I don't have to worry about me having it all together. It's not about me anyway. It's all about HIM! You don't have to have it all together. All you have to do is trust in the LORD. The Scripture in 1 Corinthians 1:27 (NIV) states, "But God chose the foolish things of the world to shame the wise; chose the weak things of the world to shame the strong." It's okay if you feel like you don't have it all together. Did you hear that? God's got you! You can be confident in God's sufficiency. Now, back to what God said to Moses. The answer God gave Moses was, "I will be with you (Exodus 3:12)." God is always with you!

Moses' second excuse was, "They won't believe me!" Like Moses, we suffer from credibility (See Exodus 3:13-17). You have to believe in yourself. Don't be arrogant! However, you must have confidence in yourself and have confidence in what

God is speaking to your spirit. Not everyone is going to agree with the mission or the instructions God gives you. When you know you have a sure word from the LORD, you have to step out in faith. Don't allow anyone to make you doubt or deviate from the plan God has given you. Keep your eyes on Him! Hebrews 12:2 says, "Looking unto Jesus, the author and finisher of our faith." Everyone's process is different. Please do yourself a favor and stop comparing your process to that of others. Just trust God! Follow God's instructions and chill! If the instruction you received is in sync with the Word of God, then do it. The instructions God gives you will always be confirmed by His written word. God will never contradict His word.

Moses' third excuse was, "What shall I do if they say that You did not appear to me (Exodus 4:2)?" The Lord commanded Moses to stretch out his stick and it became a snake. Next, Moses put his hand inside his clothing and it became leprous. This is found in Exodus 4:6-8. It's time to stop relying on validation from others. The only validation you need is that of the Holy Spirit. We have the power of God inside of us. When we abide in God's Spirit, signs, wonders, and miracles will follow those who believe His word. Luke 9:1 says, "When Jesus had called the twelve together, he gave them power and authority to drive out all demons and to cure diseases." It is not for us to say, "Look at me!" It is for God's power to be displayed within the earth and for His love to be demonstrated.

Moses' fourth excuse was, "I'm not a good public speaker." Moses had a speech impediment. The impediment was either he talked with a stutter or he had a bad lisp. Either way, Moses didn't think he was an eloquent speaker. Your thoughts might be, "I am unable to talk without spitting out my words fluidly. I can't talk without producing a consistent thought." Whatever the case might be, it doesn't matter to God. If you have to take some public speaking classes, then do so. Hire a voice coach. Do whatever it takes! If you can't afford to hire anyone for help, preach to your family, friends, or yourself. Be willing to rise to the occasion and step outside of your comfort zone. As with Moses, God will be with you and He will give you the tools needed to carry out the assignment. God had to remind Moses of His power and God gave Aaron, Moses' brother to help him be an effective leader (See Exodus 4:11-1).

I feel the fire of God being released on your tongue. As this fire is being released, God is placing His words in your mouth. Be confident in God's power and rely on your God. He will sustain you. God will never let you fail. He will anoint your speech! When people hear you talk, they will be in awe of God's power and goodness in your life. God is saying, chill out. You don't have to be afraid. I will speak to you and I will speak through you.

Moses' last excuse was, "I'm not the right person for the job. Send someone else." By this time, the LORD started to get angry with Moses. It is a sin when we willfully walk in disobedience to the things God has told us to do. We miss out on blessings by refusing the plan God has for our lives. God doesn't want us to wait to get to heaven to enjoy His blessings. No, He wants us to enjoy them now. The Scripture declares, "Now, faith is.... (Hebrews 11:1)." Right here, Right now.... God wants to use you and He wants you to receive rewards for your obedience. You my friend, yes you, you have what it takes. God knows everything about you and He didn't make a mistake when he created you! He knew everything about you including your personality, strengths and weaknesses. If you think you're not worthy, declare with me, "I have what it takes!" You can say this without hesitation due to the verse in Psalms 139:1. Say it loud and declare it with authority, "I am fearfully and wonderfully made!" Get any negative thoughts out of your head! Please cast down those thoughts of feeling inadequate. Don't allow the lies of the enemy to stop you. I prophesy, you will no longer be stuck! I prophesy, you will no longer sit by and allow life to just happen. I prophesy, you have what it takes to carry out every assignment the LORD has given to you!

My Testimony

At the beginning of last year, God gave me a prophetic word of, "No more excuses." Since last year, He keeps placing this word in my heart and bringing it back to my remembrance. Fast forward to now... God let me know the days of speaking why I can't do something is over. I echo the same to you. Stop making excuses and allow God to have His way in your life. There's so much God desires to do for you. I'm a witness that God will open the right doors for you and your gift will make room for you. You won't have to chase God's blessings. His blessings will chase you when you come into alignment with His will.

Prayer

Father, in the name of Jesus, I come to You, thanking You for being my Creator and my Lover! Help me to no longer use excuses that hinder me from walking in my purpose. I want to see myself the way You see me (healthy, whole, & victorious). Please replace any negative thoughts of my self-worth with the truth of your Word. Give me a healthy self-esteem and self-image. Amen.

CHAPTER 3

The Power of Connection

You might be thinking to yourself, "What does connection have to do with walking in your God-given purpose?" Connections have everything to do with it. The people you are connected with will either influence you in a positive or a negative way. In essence, your connections will either make you or break you. A connection is defined as a relationship in which a person, thing, or idea is linked or associated with something else according to the Oxford dictionary. If you feel stuck in your life, you might have the wrong connections. Examine your connections! Let's take a closer look at the revelation God has given me concerning connections! When I say connections, I mean God-ordained and God-given connections.

The most important connection we have is with the Holy Spirit. In order to know your purpose, you have to spend time fellowshipping with Him. Jesus understood the power of connection very well. John 10: 30 says, "I and the Father are one." We have to be one with God. When our thoughts, will, and emotions line up with Him, then it won't be a struggle to hear His voice. When we hear His voice clearly, then and only then, we will be able to identify our God-given purpose.

First, we must learn to have reliance upon the Holy Spirit. This is the number one connection we should be forming in our lives. Notice, I didn't say working towards. Often, we strive to have relationships with people, but we don't have to force it to happen in order to have a relationship with the Holy Spirit. It's a free gift that God gives to us when we accept Jesus as our Savior.

You know we all love free! We spend too much time trying to be one with people instead of being one with the LORD. Please stop listening to the voice of people and fine tune your ears to hear the voice of God's Spirit. Too often, we diminish the voice of the Holy Spirit crying out to us. Consequently, we start listening to the voice of people, which causes us to spiral out of the will of God. This only leads to confusion, which slows us down from walking in God's intended purpose. This is why before we connect with people, we must first have a connection with the Spirit of God. In John 15:4 (CEV), Jesus declares, "Stay joined to me, and I will stay joined to you, just as a branch cannot produce fruit unless it stays joined to the vine, you cannot produce fruit unless you stay joined to me." The Holy Spirit is the One who can give us our identity. The Holy Spirit is the One who causes us to be productive in our lives. When I say productive, I don't mean a lot of busy work, but He helps us to align with the purposes that will produce fruit for the Kingdom of God.

Why am I saying this? When we learn to become fully submitted to His presence, then it won't be hard to identify who we are in Christ. We spend time going to seminars, seeking other people's opinions, and hiring life coaches to figure out our purpose. When we don't get the right answers from these sources, we get angry and frustrated. Seeking direction from people instead of God will cause you to be stuck. Here we go again, like the children of Israel, stuck in the desert. We take one more lap around the mountain. I hear the LORD saying, "You have dwelt long enough at this mountain (Deuteronomy 1:6).

I prophesy, "It's time for you to get off the mountain!" To me, a mountain represents whatever barriers in our lives that appears formidable. When these false expectations appearing real (FEAR) manifest in our minds, the Holy Spirit will rise up on the inside our spirits to remind us the truth of God's word. You don't have to stay stuck in life! With the Holy Spirit leading and guiding you, God has already provided a way of escape for you. The Holy Spirit wants you to seek Him for revelation. Right now, at this very moment, ask the Holy Spirit to show you how the Father sees you. Secondly, ask the Holy Spirit to reveal your divine purpose. The Father is eagerly waiting for you to cry out to Him, so that He can download revelation to you.

When we establish an appropriate relationship with the Holy Spirit, it won't be hard for us to have the right connections with others. It saddens me to see many people in the body of Christ striving hard to be connected to certain big names in ministry. Our number one priority and calling is to be connected to HIM. The Holy Spirit is our everything! When prioritizing people over God's Spirit, it grieves the Holy Spirit. We must stop chasing after people and learn to passionately pursue God. Let's become determined in our hearts that we will be God chasers.

But seek ye first the kingdom of God, and His righteousness; and all these things shall be added unto you (Matthew 6:33). If you desire promotion, seek God. However, we shouldn't be seeking God for promotion only. We should seek God because we genuinely love Him. God loves you with an everlasting love. Therefore, we should reciprocate the same love, affection, and devotion in return. Again, people can't promote you! God is the only one who can bring increase into your life! We can't believe the hype and fall prey to the lies of the enemy that promotion comes from who you know (people, that is). Some people think by chasing after Christian celebrities, or if they connect with a particular famous person, then they will become famous.

I am quickly reminded of the Scriptures in Psalm 75:6-7, "For promotion cometh neither from the east, nor from the west, nor from the south. But God is the judge: he putted down one, and setteth up another." I'm so grateful to know that if I want a promotion in my life that all I have to do is ask the Father. If you desire promotion, then humbly ask your Heavenly Father. We can boldly ask the Father! You desire but do not have, so you kill. You covet but you cannot get what you want, so you quarrel and fight. You do not have because you do not ask God. When you ask, you do not receive, because you ask with wrong motives, that you may spend what you get on your pleasures (James 4:2-3).

When you ask God for promotion, make sure your motives are pure. You shouldn't desire a promotion to be in the spotlight so people can see you or for your own selfish desires and ambitions. We must be motivated by love. Whatever elevation the Father allows us to obtain we should always give God the glory and not ourselves. We should always give credit to the Father. When people ask, how did this happen for you, we should humbly say, it was God who made this possible for me. We should always point people to Jesus! Without the help of the Holy Spirit, there's no way I could be writing this book. It's through God that I live and have my being! This is an example of giving God the glory and honor.

When we have a true connection with the Holy Spirit, we soon realize, without a shadow of a doubt, nothing is too hard for God and with Him we can do the impossible. The thing we have to get in our minds is when we feel like we are being overlooked or cheated out of a position. God is allowing it to happen for a reason. Don't focus on the closed doors. Ask God to show you what He's trying to teach you. I'm learning when there's a closed door or a door that won't open, God is rerouting us to a bigger and better door of opportunity. Let me reiterate this. We have to trust GOD. We have to keep our eyes on Jesus and not people. Why? Let me say this, LOUD and CLEAR, seek God for promotion and not man! God will never overlook you! When the appointed time comes, He will give you elevation.

You don't have to chase after anyone to get an upgrade in your life. You don't have to lower your standards to get an upgrade in your life. One thing to always remember is this. If man gives you a promotion, then you will have to jump through hoops to keep it. When God gives you a promotion, it's yours, period! No one can take it away from you. The Father loves to bless His children with good gifts. God loves to bring elevation to His chosen people. Especially, those who people think will never be anything or those who people have deemed to not have the right qualities or skill sets. Wow, this is shouting news for me. God will take the underdog and make them the top dog.

1 Corinthians 1:27 says, "But God has chosen the foolish things of the world to confound the wise, and God has chosen the weak things of the world to put to shame the things which are mighty." Hello, underdog, God is calling you to

rise up! It's time for you to come out of obscurity. God wanted me to remind you that when you become connected to HIM, He will bring you out! It doesn't matter who comes against what God has spoken to you! Renounce the word curses people try to pronounce over you. Shake off everything that was said over you that doesn't line up with God's Word concerning you! God wanted me to remind you of this fact. The fact is God has destined you for greatness! Lastly, the people who are fighting against you might not want to promote you! Rest assured, my brother or my sister, God will make your enemies your foot stools. He will use the same people who said you couldn't, can't or you won't as a springboard to launch you into your destiny. I hear the words, ELEVATION! Get ready for it! God will bring promotion to you in the face of your naysayers and He will use your critics to catapult you into destiny. If you don't believe me, let's look at the book of Esther.

As the book of Esther starts out, we see Esther has a first cousin whose name is Mordecai. After the death of Esther's mother and father, Mordecai adopted the beautiful Esther and raised her in his home as his own daughter. In your personal life, you might not have a mother or father, but God will connect you to spiritual parents who will love you and treat you as their own. God isn't a respecter of persons. However, He is a respecter of faith. What God did for Esther, He will do the same for you.

Let me get back to my original thought. In Esther chapter 3, Haman develops a plot to annihilate the Jewish people. Haman utterly despises Mordecai. Haman hated Mordecai and the Jewish people. Poor Haman! He comes up with every plot imaginable to kill Mordecai and the Jewish people. However, we know Haman wasn't a match with the power of God. The Scriptures states in Romans 8:31 (NIV), "What, then, shall we say in response to these things? If God is for us, who can be against us?" Let me take this moment to encourage you! Stop focusing on the people who are coming against you and the people who want to see you fail. Start focusing on the one true God who loves you and absolutely adores you! Let this fact sink into your spirit. Their negative thoughts, negative opinions, and negative behavior against you doesn't matter. God is on your side and He is your biggest cheerleader.

Let me say this again! God is on your side and no one or no plan of the enemy will be able to work against you! How quickly do we forget this verse in Romans 8:31? You have the Creator of the universe fighting for you. You have a heavenly host fighting on your behalf. Like God protected Mordecai, He will protect YOU! Your naysayers or enemies aren't a match against the power of God. You have an undefeated champion fighting on your behalf. You can be at peace! Just knowing God has never lost a battle and He never will. God will always be undefeated. As God was with Mordecai and Esther, He will be with you. Selah! Now as an act of faith, start thanking God for the victories He's about to bring into your life. There's going to be a brighter day in your life. You will soon begin to see God's hand at work in your life.

Now, back to Mordecai and how God delivered him and his people. We discover God usesd Queen Esther to save her people. The lovely Queen Esther reveals the wicked plan of the evil Haman. God exposed Haman's plan to the King. The plot Haman developed against Mordecai, God reversed it. This is shouting news! God will reverse the evil plans people have tried to set against you. He will turn it around for you! Point blank. Period. Genesis 50:20 (NIV) says, "You intended to harm me, but God intended it for good to accomplish what is now being done, the saving of many lives." In the book of Esther, we read, Haman died on the gallows he had built for Mordecai. Not only did Haman die, but also his ten sons died. After Haman's death, Mordecai becomes second in command to King Ahasuerus (Read, Esther, 8:1-2 and 10:3). Through God's protection, Israel is rescued. My friend, God wants to do the same for you. Whoever is coming against you, God will rescue you from every evil scheme of your enemies. The Scripture declares the LORD will make your enemies your footstool. God will use the same people who tried to curse you to bless you!

Like Esther had Mordecai to assist her in discovery of her purpose, God wants to bring the right people in your life that will assist you. People who will genuinely love you! People who will provide the tools needed to get you to your next level in God! It's time to level up! God wants to clearly show you these God-ordained people, but you can't be afraid to let the "right" people get close to you. Before we go any further, please pray. Ask the Father to heal your heart where people have caused heartbreak to you. You have to have an open heart. I know people may have hurt you in the past, but you have to trust God for the right connections.

At this second, you might be thinking, "I feel so alone and isolated." You might even be discouraged. Cheer up my friend! I have good news for you. You are never alone. God is always with you! God declares in His Word that He will never leave you or forsake you. He loves you with an everlasting love. No one, no critic, or even a nay-sayer can affect the love God has for you. The other good news I want to share with you is you don't have to remain isolated from people either. In times past, people may have hurt you or let you down. Stop focusing on the past, and start believing God for a better present. God will bring trust-worthy people to you who will cover you in prayer and encouragement. No man or woman should be an island unto themselves.

Ecclesiastes 4:9-10 says, "Two are better than one; because they have a good reward for their labour. For if they fall, the one will lift up his fellow: but woe to him that is alone when he falleth, for he hath not another to help him up." Jesus wasn't a renegade. He chose the twelve to walk with him in his ministry. Even Jesus had to face betrayal with Judas. Jesus knew Judas was going to betray him, but loved him in spite of the betrayal. No one is exempt from being hurt in relationships. I'm not saying to be reckless. God will teach us how to guard our hearts. When I say guard, I don't mean we build walls to keep people out. We have to ask the Holy Spirit to help us to distinguish who's who in our lives.

For example, you don't have to allow everyone to come within your inner circle and tell them everything about you. Apply wisdom and prayer. Be careful what you share with people who come into your life. Ask the Holy Spirit what position this person holds in your life? Can they be trusted? God, is this person sent by You or the enemy? Do you have peace about the person that is trying to connect with you? If you get a check in your spirit about a person, or a feeling that something isn't right about a person, don't ignore it. Normally, this is the Holy Spirit trying to warn you about that particular person. Don't override the check, but press into the Holy Spirit to show you what it is about this person that is not right. Once the Holy Spirit shows you, bless them and keep it moving. Don't give that relationship a second thought. In everything we should always be seeking God's peace. If there's no peace, I admonish you to let it go!

We are commanded to love. Love doesn't mean you have to allow people to abuse you or take advantage of you. You have to set the appropriate boundaries in relationships. Love says, "Father, forgive them for they know not what they do." This is exactly what Jesus did when he was betrayed and what he said as he lay dying upon the cross. You choose to love people despite their shortcomings. However, you don't have to allow those people to be in your inner circle and let them treat you any kind of way. You deserve to be valued and treated as a son/daughter of the Most High God. You are royalty! Another thing, when people treat you wrong, it gives you wisdom of how to treat people the right way. You experience how it feels to be hurt. Don't repeat the cycle by treating people with the same pain that was inflicted upon you. No, choose to break the cycle of hurt by loving people the right way. You might say, "I tried allowing people to come into my life, but I always get hurt." Stop speaking word curses over your life. Declare and decree with me, "God will place the right people in my life. People who will love me the right way!" The LORD designed us to be connected to others and to have healthy relationships. First, God wants us to be one with His Spirit; however, He wants us to learn how to establish connections with other people. It's important for us to have interactions with our fellow brothers and sisters in Christ Jesus. I know you're thinking, "How do I know who to connect with?" The Holy Spirit will show you who's who, the people who genuinely love you, and the people God has called to your life! Everyone is not called to be apart of your life.

I'm sure people have treated you wrong. As a result, you don't have to take matters into your own hands. Like Mordecai, let God fight your battles where people have wronged you. You don't have to try to get even with people and give them a piece of your mind, LOL. You can trust God. Vengeance belongs to HIM. God will take care of the people that are coming for you! You won't have to do anything, but worship God. When you consecrate yourself in prayer and worship unto God, He will set up ambushes against your enemies. If you don't believe me, read about King Jehoshaphat in 2nd Chronicles 20:22. This is a great reminder of God's faithfulness! God fought the battle for King Jehoshaphat which means, He will do the same for me and you! Our warfare is never against people, but we have an enemy. Ephesians 6:12 states it best, "For we wrestle not against flesh against and blood, but against principalities, against powers, against the rulers of the darkness of this world, against spiritual wickedness in high places." In order to use effective warfare strategies, we have to use the weapons of prayer, fasting, the Word and worship to counteract the attacks of the enemies.

I want to tell you this. Not everyone will be happy about the successes God gives you. Consequently, you can't allow it and a lack of support to deter you from the path to greatness. Everyone is not assigned to walk with you in your destiny. Amos 3:3 expresses, "Can two walk together, except they be agreed?" You need people in your life who will be in agreement with your destiny! The wrong connections in your life can hinder your purpose. Some people don't want to see you blessed! They will smile in your face and behind your back, they will be try to block or speak word curses against your destiny. That's why you have to build in secret and watch who you share your vision with. Let me declare this over you by God's power, "No weapon formed against you shall prosper! No word curses spoken over you will be able to hinder your destiny! You are blessed! You walk in divine purpose!"

As you continue to walk in purpose, one thing you always need to do is pray about every connection you have in your life. God doesn't want you to be deceived in any area of your life. Ask Him to reveal the motives of the people who are a part of your life. Be bold! Say, "LORD should this person be in my life or should this person not be in my life?" However, when you ask, be prepared to receive some hard truths. John 8:32 says, "And ye shall know the truth, and the truth shall make you free." God will clearly show you who is for you and who is against you. Once He reveals the truth to you, you might get angry, cry, and become disappointed. You can't allow it to deter you or hinder you from moving forward! Don't be surprised when without warning, people begin to walk out of your life. Let them go! Don't try to chase after them and wonder what happened? Just know God responded to your prayer. He's protecting you! You might have to walk alone for a period of time. Continue to be steadfast! Please, keep moving forward and don't look back. At the right time, God will bring the right people in your life. Declare with me, "God is bringing the right people in my life. People who will pray for me, encourage me, and who will help strengthen my walk with God." Now, your thought might be, "How will I be able to identify the right people?" Pray without ceasing! Stay alert! Keep a watchful eye through prayer! Stay focused on Jesus! The Holy Spirit will bring illumination as to who is a destiny destroyer and who is a destiny blessing! Pray!

Lastly, the Holy Spirit will give you discernment. Discernment is the ability to judge which things of a particular kind are good and which are bad (Collins dictionary). I prophesy, God is releasing wisdom and the spirit of discernment upon you. You will no longer be fooled by people who are destiny destroyers. I prophesy, you are going to have the right connections with those who are going to help birth your God-given purpose and potential.

My testimony

I have to say this. I am grateful for my entire family! I don't want to call names. I might get in trouble if I leave someone out, lol. They know who they are. They have always been supportive of me. I wouldn't be able to write this book without their love and encouragement. Now, back to my testimony. This year, the year of 2020, God has brought many powerful men and women of God into my life. Talk about iron sharpening iron. Last year, I felt stuck and stagnant, but this year God has birthed many spiritual gifts within me. I am surrounded by my company of Prophets, who encourage, push me to go higher in God and pray for me. I am praying, preaching, teaching, and prophesying at a greater capacity. Lastly, through my connection with Prophetess Kimberly Moses, God used her to push me to write this book and to develop me as a leader. Next, I met two other great women of God who are assisting with my ministry development. Chile, Godly connections are everything. Honestly, I don't want to leave anyone out. With this being said, I am grateful for everyone who has assisted in my personal, spiritual, and business growth/development. I wouldn't be the person I am today without their help. I love you all! Thank you for allowing God to use you to make me a better woman! I am eternally grateful! I do not share my testimony to brag or to boast on myself, but I want to testify of God's goodness and faithfulness. Dare to believe God for more! God has destined you for greatness.

Prayer

LORD, I thank you, that every good and perfect gift comes from You! Oh LORD, You created us to have fellowship with you and with others. Allow us to be one with Your Holy Spirit. Next, allow us to have God-given relationships; the relationships that give glory and honor to You. I ask You to help us to clearly discern the people that are sent by You and to let go of the people not ordained by You. In Jesus Name, Amen.

CHAPTER 4

Overcoming Fear & Knowing Who You Are In Christ

I hear the Spirit of the Lord saying, "It's time for you to come forward and allow the Lord to use you for His glory." You have been hidden in the cave far too long! The time is now! It's time for you to drop the safety nets! It's time for you to have a seat at the table. You weren't created to be hidden in the background! You were created to be an influencer! You are a decision maker! No longer will God allow you to be comfortable with sitting on the side-lines and just settling for whatever is handed to you or what people think you should be doing. God wants to strategically place you. The Spirit of God is blowing fresh winds of change over your destiny. "Today, if you will choose to hear my voice," says the Lord, "And choose to not harden your heart against the things the Holy Spirit wants to reveal to you." He will perform a new thing in you! At this time and at this moment! It's a new day! It's a new hour! God is opening doors for the ones who have been overlooked, under-booked, and those who are deemed unworthy by society. The choice is yours! Are you ready to embrace the new?

First, all God wants is a yes from you and your obedience. God wants you to have a courageous heart like Joshua. As we recall, Moses mentored Joshua to become the leader of the Israelites after his death. Joshua trusted God for the process and we have to do the same. It won't be an overnight process. However, God will bring us to an expected end. I hope you're ready like me to begin this wonderful journey with the Holy Spirit. The Father wants you and me to trust Him as He leads us away from that which is familiar. It's time to launch into the deep! It's time to walk into uncharted territory. It's time for us to shake off our fears. But you might be thinking, "NO WAY!" You just don't realize how hard it is for me to overcome being fearful and being controlled by FEAR. Yes, I do! I understand how crippling fear can be quite well! If I can do it, you can too! I want to resound the charge in your ears that God gave Joshua.

In Joshua 1:9, the LORD said to Joshua, " Have I not commanded you? Be strong and of a good courage; be not afraid, neither be thou dismayed: for the LORD thy God is with thee whithersoever thou goest." Did you hear that? Where you go, the LORD is with you! Things may catch us off guard, but nothing catches God by surprise. He is all wise, all seeing, all powerful, and all knowing God! Whew, that takes the pressure off of me and you. We can rest and be fully assured that no matter what path we take, God has it all figured out. All we have to do is to trust HIM and to rely on HIM. Be still and listen for God's voice guiding you along the way. You can stand in complete confidence that God is always with you.

Here's your shouting moment! Are you ready? Selah, pause and think on this! You have the Creator of the universe with you in every circumstance. The God, who spoke the world into existence! The God, who declared, "Let there be light" and the light began to shine bright through the darkness. The God, who created every living creature upon the face of the earth. The God, who separated the dry land from the waters. The God who created the sun, moon, and the stars. More importantly, the God, the same God, who created you and me. The ONE, and Only God, who made us in HIS image and likeness. My beloved friend, you aren't an accident! You were created for purpose and to be used for the glory of God. I don't care how weird you think your personality might be. I don't care how many people have made fun, ridiculed, or laughed at you. Yeah you, God has chosen you for the job!

The thing I want to point out is it's the Holy Spirit doing the work. However, you must drop your fears and allow Him to work through you. Who cares if you might sing off key? Who cares if you might laugh at every joke, even the ones that aren't really funny? Who cares if you feel like you're always the last one getting picked? Who cares if you have a loud or a quiet demeanor? Who cares if people think you're crazy? Who cares if you can't read or write very well? Who cares if you aren't an eloquent speaker? The bottom line is God wants to use you!

What I love about God is that you don't have to be a scholar. All God wants is your yes! Will you be willing to step outside the box? When I say box, I mean the boundaries and limitations you have put on yourself. Or it might be, the limitations and restrictions that people have placed upon you. It's time for you to shake those things off. I declare by the Spirit of God, "No longer shall you be hindered by a narrow viewpoint of yourself and the negative opinions of people! No longer shall you be afraid, tortured, and bound by the Spirit of Fear!" I hear the chains breaking off your life. God has created so many wonderful things for you! He wants you to renew your mind to see yourself the way He sees you! In God, the possibilities for your life are endless. With God, He will remove every glass ceiling the enemy has tried to place over you. I want to leave you with these words from the Scripture in Matthew 19:26, "With God all things are possible and nothing shall be impossible to those who believe."

One of the crippling things the enemy will try to use against you is FEAR. The spirit of fear will try to derail and block your destiny. Don't allow FEAR to paralyze you and try to render you null and void. If you let it, this spirit will try to shut you down. Don't allow FEAR to put a muzzle on your mouth. Cry aloud and spare not! Boldly declare, the words, the creativity, and the purpose God has placed within you. Right now, by the power of Jesus Christ, you will begin to take authority over FEAR. I want to encourage you like Paul encouraged Timothy. Let's look at it together and repeat it together over and over and over again. I want this Scripture to take root into your heart. Let it become a living word in your life. Say it LOUD with me! Here we go, "FOR GOD hath not given us the spirit of fear, but of power, and of love and of a sound mind." This is a powerful Scripture and declaration found in 2 Timothy 1:7. Beloved, you have got to believe this with all your heart, mind, and your entire being. You might feel fear, but you don't have to allow fear to control you and cause you to become immobilized.

Let's go a little further and break down the Scripture Paul wrote to his protégée Timothy in 2 Timothy 1:7. I'm sure you hear this Scripture quoted all the time. However, it's important for us to truly understand what it means in order to receive the revelation God is trying to give us. Let's dig a little deeper. To accurately understand Paul's writing, we must first define, FEAR. Fear is derived from the Greek word Phobos. The word origin is from phebomai, which means to be put to flight. The other words to define fear are alarm, fright, dread, or terror. It's compatible with our English word "Phobia." A phobia is an extreme or irrational fear or aversion to something. Let's dive into 2 Timothy 1:7. Fear doesn't come from God. Fear is a demonic spirit. Its job is to render you ineffective and to keep you from walking in your purpose. Fear will cause you to be spiritually blind. It blinds you from knowing who you are in Christ Jesus. That's why Paul declared to Timothy, "God hasn't given you a spirit of fear." Get angry at the devil! It's time for you to reclaim your life. It's time for you to take back everything the enemy tried to steal from you!!!

Are you ready to reclaim your life? You reclaim your life by knowing the power and authority God has given to you through Jesus, our Savior. One of the things you must know is you have POWER! Yes, you.... God has given you POWER! You aren't weak, helpless and you don't have to remain afraid!!! You don't have to be stuck!!! Refuse to settle!!! Be determined to not allow FEAR to control you! Why? Again, you have POWER! God has deposited HIS Spirit within you! The Holy Spirit gives you POWER! You aren't powerless, my beloved, you are powerful!

Power is defined as the ability to act or produce an effect according to the Merriam Webster dictionary. This power isn't based upon your strength and ability. This power comes from God alone. It comes from the help of the Holy Spirit! You have the Holy Spirit living on the inside of you. He is the one who gives you power! He is the One who sustains you. He is the One who helps you to overcome fear: The HOLY SPIRIT. Romans 6:10 declares it this way, "The Spirit of God, who raised Jesus from the dead, lives in you." This is shouting news! God will give life to the things in your life that seem lifeless. He will elevate you and equip you to do the impossible! The Holy Spirit on the inside of you gives you the power and authority to trample over any demonic spirit that tries to steal and kill your destiny! Luke 10:19 declares, "Behold, I give you the authority to trample on serpents and scorpions, and over all the power of the enemy: and nothing shall by any means hurt you." Raise up your bowed down head! You aren't defeated and you don't have to stay bound by fear. YOU HAVE POWER! Pick up your sword (the Word of God). Fight for your freedom! Jesus died and shed His blood to make you free. Freedom is your inheritance!

The next gift God has given to you is LOVE. You must know that God loves you with an everlasting love. His love for you is perfect! His love for you is complete. There is nothing you can do to earn His love or diminish the love God has for you! What a great revelation! God loves you. Point Blank. Period! You are the apple of HIS eye! Your worth and value are greater than any gemstone or rare jewel upon this earth! All you have to do is accept His Love. Repeat after me, "Father God, I accept your love!" Now, that settles it! Fear can't stand in the way of God's love! 1 John 4:18 states, "There is no fear in love; but perfect love casteth out fear: because fear has torment. He that feareth is not made perfect in love." When you begin to focus on God's ultimate love for you, FEAR has to go! Every time fear tries to arise in your life to overtake you, start thinking about Jesus and His completed work on the cross. He loves and cares for you. Repeat after me, "FEAR, you have no authority in my life! I choose to not allow you to cripple me! I choose to believe God! I will walk in faith and freedom! I have been made complete through God's love for me."

Whatever the fear is that is trying to keep you bound, I want to encourage you through the victory Jesus has provided for you! You are more than victorious. No longer shall you allow the enemy to muzzle your mouth! No longer shall you remain comfortable by playing it safe! No longer will you be happy with the status quo. God hasn't called you to be complacent or to settle. You beloved, you were created to shine bright for the glory of God. Isaiah 43:7 (NLT) says, "Bring all who claim me as their God, for I have made them for my glory. It was I who created them." Good news! You were created for a purpose. I want to sound the alarm in your spirit. You Got This! By your blood bought right, FEAR has to release its crippling effects from your life. Proverbs 28:1 states, "The righteous are bold as a lion." Within you, you have the DNA of a lion. Jesus is the lion of Judah. Yes, you... God, through His son Jesus, has given you a spirit that is BOLD and courageous.

I want to remind you of the words God spoke to Joshua when he was elevated as the leader over Israel. In Joshua 1:9, God commanded the Israelite leader, "Be Strong and Courageous! Do not be afraid; do not be discouraged, the LORD your GOD will be with you wherever you go." My friend, let us resound these words together, "Be STRONG and Be COURAGEOUS!" We don't have to be afraid. We might feel fear, but we don't have to allow it to control us! We don't have to back down! We don't have to run! Why? God is with us! Wherever we go, HE goes! Our Father is right here with us! God is the One who is empowering us to get the job done. We might feel alone! However, that's FEAR: "False Evidence Appearing Real." It's an illusion and not our reality. We have to dig in with faith and know without any doubt, God is there! God's Spirit, God's presence, and God's power is always with us!

Matthew 28:20 declares, "He is with you always, even to the end of the age." My personal testimony is, God is a deliverer. If I listened to the fears that have tried to sideline me in my life, you wouldn't be reading this book now. I want this to be an encouragement for you that with God, all things are possible. You can do anything when you put God first! What I love about God is He isn't a respecter of persons. If He did it for me, guess what? He can do the same for you. All God desires is your faith. The faith that says, "LORD, no matter what, I trust you!" I have been tormented by the fear of public speaking, meeting new people, driving, etc. At one point in my life, I was afraid of my own shadow, lol. This is real talk! However, I have made the decision to obtain God's best for my life and I refuse to allow fear to hinder me. I choose to believe God at all costs no matter how uncomfortable the journey might become and to follow God in faith. Likewise, if you want victory over fear you have to obey God and do what He is speaking to you. Will it be easy? Sadly, the answer is no, but the rewards of your obedience with be well worth it.

One thing I know for sure is God will never let you down. He doesn't lie! He will never leave you or forsake you! Can I get a witness? In my own life, God has always been there for me and He's always caused me to triumph in every challenge! One thing I realize is God is my vindicator! He is the One fighting on my behalf. He is the One going before me to make every crooked path straight. He is the one who is enabling me to carry out the assignments and tasks He has given to me. It's liberating to know it's God who is doing the work! I said all of this to say, you can live your life in the liberty and freedom that Jesus has provided for you despite all of the things that may seem to be crippling in your life.

You might even feel stuck and trapped by fear! This is not your permanent position! It's time for you to shift and to trust God beyond what you see with your natural eyes. Beloved, there is a way of escape! YOU don't have to be bound or rendered immobile by FEAR. You may say, yeah but... it's easier said than done. I want to leave you with this thought. God can do the impossible in your life. God wants to show Himself strong in your life. If you don't believe me, the Scripture states, "For the eyes of the LORD run to and fro throughout the whole earth, to shew Himself strong in the lives of them whose heart is perfect toward Him." In other words, if you're loyal to God, He will be loyal to you! He wants to make your life a testimony through His power and His faithfulness! Stop thinking you aren't worthy to receive His promises! You are enough! You have what it takes to be everything God said you could be and who He wants you to become. Fear can't stop you! Fear can't block you from God's blessing! That's why we have to keep our minds renewed through the word of God.

The third thing I want to look at is God has given you a sound mind. Your thoughts, emotions and your decision making processes might be all over the place. Don't allow FEAR (False

Evidence Appearing Real) to dictate your destiny. That's why you can't be led by your feelings and emotions. In order for you to have a sound mind, a mind that doesn't waver when things go the opposite of God's word. You have to put on the helmet of salvation. This helmet helps to protect your mind when the enemy tries to bombard your mind with mental attacks. The first thing you must do is guard your mind. Above all else, guard your heart, for everything you do flows from it (Proverbs 4:23). The enemy fights you the hardest in your mind. If he can plant negative thoughts in your mind and you start to believe it, then he can try to defeat you. Most of the battles we fight are in our minds. That's why it's important for us to safeguard our minds. You might ask, "How do I do this?" You do this by keeping your mind renewed through God's word.

I love this Scripture! Psalm 1:1-2 says, "Blessed is the man that walks not in the counsel of the ungodly, nor stands in the way of sinner, nor sits in the seat of the scornful. But his delight is in the law of the LORD; and in his law doth he meditate day and night." The word meditate means to ponder or to think. Constantly think or focus on the word of God! This is a sure way to develop a sound mind.

Refuse to allow the enemy to take punk shots in your mind. You don't have to believe his lies! You don't have to take everything he tries to throw at you! I have good news for you! God has given you authority over the enemy. By the blood that Jesus has shed for you, you will no longer be bound by the lies of the enemy in your mind! Christ has redeemed you! He wants to make you free from everything that tries to hold you hostage. It breaks now! God declares in His word, "You have a sound mind." You don't have to freak out or think you're going crazy! You're not losing your mind! In fact, you're gaining your mind. You're taking back what the enemy tried to steal from you.

As an act of faith, repeat this declaration with me! Shout this out-loud, "GOD HAS GIVEN ME A SOUND MIND!" Sound means your mind is solid. You have a mind that cannot be hindered or shaken by the enemy! Your mind is protected and secured by Jesus. You have the mind of Christ: a mind that can think logically. A mind that isn't controlled by fear. A mind that is stable when everything around you is chaotic. You can be at peace. Isaiah 26:3 says, "Thou will keep him in perfect peace, whose mind is stayed on thee: because he trusted in thee." Jesus promised, if you keep your mind on Him, He will keep you in perfect peace. This is another way to keep your mind safeguarded. Please keep your mind focused on Jesus and not on what is going on around you. Do you feel God's presence surrounding you with peace? There's nothing in this world that compares to God's peace. Protect the peace that God gives to you at all costs. After reading this chapter, I hope you are ready to reclaim your mind and conquer your fear!

My testimony

Most of my life has been ridden with and controlled by fear. I'm grateful to God for not allowing me to stay bound by fear. This year God is stretching me! I'm praying for people and teaching the Word on prayer calls. Another thing God has done in my life to break fear is He has me going live on social media creating videos and prophesying to random people. If you're serious about overcoming fear, God will put you to the test. Get ready to launch into the deep. Again, you don't have to be afraid. God will be there with you to guide you through the process.

Prayer

Father, I thank You for your Son, Jesus! I thank You, LORD, that You died that we might live! Thank You, LORD, for redeeming us from every curse of the law. Empower us by your Holy Spirit to only be bold and courageous! Holy Spirit, I ask You to help us to walk in the liberty that Jesus gave us to be free in every area of our lives. The freedom from mental strongholds (fear, doubt, and unbelief)- anything that would keep us bound in our minds. Help us to keep our minds focused on you! Help us to safeguard our minds through Your infallible Word. In Jesus Name, Amen.

CHAPTER 5

Take God At His Word

In order for you to rise above your circumstances, you simply have to take God at His word. You become unstoppable when you learn to take God at His word! It's more than saying you believe God. You have to know deep within your heart that God is working all things together for your good. You must possess the mindset of no matter what's currently going in your life, God has a plan for you and simply choose to believe God against all odds! We have to adopt the same demeanor as Mary, "Lord, be unto me according to your word" (Luke 1:38 ESV). This knowing goes beyond what you think or imagine with your natural comprehension! It's a knowing that God will do what He said He will do in your life. No matter who comes or goes, no matter who disagrees with the vision God has given you, you may have to walk alone! That's okay. Guess what? God is with you! You are never alone! God is walking with you and He's fighting for you! Please stand on God's Word and do not waiver at His promises.

I want to take this moment to encourage you! Keep Going! Keep Moving Forward! Keep Trusting God! Don't you dare allow the enemy to make you doubt God's promises for you! Shake off every spirit of sabotage and delay that is trying to hold you hostage! There is a way of escape for you. You might say, "Yeah, you have no idea of the things I've gone through and yet nothing has changed for me." I feel trapped and I feel as though God has forsaken me. Take heart and be of good cheer! God has not forsaken you! The mere fact that I am penning these words is an indicator that God hasn't forgotten about you.

At one point in my life, I felt the same way. As I type, with tears streaming from my eyes, not tears of sadness, but tears of joy! I have to stop and take a moment to reflect on God's goodness and His faithfulness! Like you, I've felt trapped. I felt hopeless!!! I want to testify that little by little, God is bringing deliverance to me. He is showing me my divine purpose and opening supernatural doors for me. Is everything in my life perfect? No, it's not! However, I can testify that God will bring you out! He's a promise keeper! I'm a witness of His delivering power!

When you feel as though you have reached a breaking point and the enemy is trying to make you think you're going to lose your mind, don't give into the enemy's lies. Now, isn't the time for you to turn your back on God! Stop yielding to the temptation to quit! Can't you see the small glimmer of light shining through the darkness in your life? If you can't physically see it, see it with the eyes of your faith! There's a breakthrough just around the corner for you! With the voice of faith, recite this Scripture aloud and hold fast to what you say. The Scripture is, "there is nothing too hard for God!" This is the same Scripture

God declared to Jeremiah when Israel was taken into Babylonian captivity. This was a time when everything seemed hopeless for Israel. Despite the hopelessness and despair, Jeremiah obeyed God's instructions. Jeremiah believed God beyond what he could see with his limited view. God will come through for you! God will always rescue HIS people. We have to pray during the dark periods of life. We must ask the Father to help us to trust Him when things don't make sense. Jeremiah believed. We have to believe! Let these words resound loud and clear in your mind and spirit. I want you to recite this Scripture again and believe what you're saying. Here it is...God simply said in Jeremiah 32:27, "Behold, I am the LORD, the God of all flesh: is there anything too hard for me?" Dig deeper!!! Did you hear that? There's nothing in your life that's too hard for God to handle. There's nothing in your life that is beyond God's sovereignty! He is GOD! Period!

Please take time to cultivate your relationship with God. As you spend time seeking Him, it will help you to trust God in a greater measure. I don't care what has happened in your life. It doesn't matter how much time has passed for

God's promises to be manifested over your life. God can! God will do the impossible in your life. You might have people taunting you with insults. Or simply making fun of you due to what appears to be limitations. Did you hear what I just said? It appears to be that God has forgotten you. It appears you are stuck in a repetitive cycle. It appears... You feel in the blank as to what is holding you back from believing the promises God has spoken to you.

I'm not writing this to tickle your ears or to give you an emotional hype. I'm writing this to stir up your faith. I want you to have faith to believe and receive God's promises. Did you know your promises are tailored especially for you? No one can access the promises God has laid out for you, but you. However, those promises can be forfeited. This can happen by doubt and unbelief. It can occur by disobeying God's commandments and willfully sinning against God. The Biblical example that sticks out to me is that of King Saul. He lost his kingship due to him not obeying God's instructions. This can be found in 1 Samuel 15. Let's set our hearts towards God and choose to obey HIM. It's time to say, "Lord, I trust you!" Now, that you have acknowledged this truth, we have to shift our perspective! We have to SEE through the lenses of faith. Faith comes by hearing God's word. You must be willing to do more than just hear it, but you must be willing to put God's Word into practice. Whatever instruction God gives you, say, "Yes," and obey HIS voice. Change doesn't occur in our lives without an action. The next thing you must ask yourself is this question. How bad do you want it? Your Joy? Your Peace? Your Destiny? Your Health? Your God ordained promises? Confess it out loud, whatever you are believing God to do in your life. What is hindering you from moving forward? Boldly declare, "I will no longer allow this_____ to define me! No longer will I accept this limitation as a permanent position in life." Now that you have accepted this truth, your time as a caterpillar has expired. The LORD wants you to know, "Your wings are ready!" It's time to fly with the wings of faith! It's time to walk into a new season!

Our Heavenly Father is amazing. I love how He uses those whom the world laughs at and criticizes —those who people try to label as an underdog.

God loves to bring elevation to those who people have discarded. I want to increase your faith! A faith that goes beyond knowing, but a faith that believes, a faith that transcends any natural limitations or impossibilities. Let's look at biblical examples of people who God elevated in spite of their naysayers. These heroes and heroines of faith refused to settle. They believed God against all odds! They dug in their heels with faith being their anchor and wouldn't let go of God's promises until the promises were manifested. But first, I need to set a biblical foundation for faith.

Faith is more than a feeling. Your feelings can trick you. Feelings and emotions will cause you to be on cloud nine one day and rock bottom the next day. Feelings aren't faith. Your feelings can lie to you. If you allow your feelings to lead you, you could potentially miss God's promises! Being guided by your feelings will cause you to be unstable. You will be on an emotional roller coaster. God doesn't want you to be see-sawing through life. He wants you to be controlled by His Word and His spirit, which produces stability. This is faith! Faith is choosing to believe God when your situation doesn't "appear" to be favorable. Faith is the full assurance that God will do what He declares in HIS Word. God wants us to be tempered by His Word. It's a knowing that goes beyond what we see with our natural eyes. It is believing God's Word. His promises are 'yes and amen' to those who believe. You might be thinking, "Yeah, yeah.... Well, Terra, how do I develop faith?" The Scripture in Romans 10:17 reads, "So then faith comes by hearing, and hearing by the word of God." Confess it. This is how faith is established. Stability will occur when you constantly meditate on the Scriptures.

Psalm 1:2-3 says, "But His delight is in the law of the LORD: and his law doth he meditate day and night. And he shall be like a tree planted by the rivers of water, that bringeth forth his fruit in his season; his leaf also shall not wither; and whatsoever he doth shall prosper." Another powerful Scripture I want us to look at is Joshua 1:8 (BSB), "This Book of the Law must not depart from your mouth; you are to recite it day and night so that you may be careful to everything written in it. For then you will prosper and succeed in all you do." God wants you to prosper and become successful. He wants you to rise above your adverse circumstances. You aren't defined by your current status in life. You are defined by God's Word! You might be thinking in your mind, "That's easy for you to say. You don't realize the extreme problems that are occurring in my life. You don't realize how long this has been happening." I want to encourage you: God knows! He feels your pain and understands your disappointments. Beloved, God is faithful! God will give you double honor for your shame and bring restoration into your life.

God is waiting to bless you! He wants to turn your life around and make you a testimony of His power. In Jeremiah 29:11 (NIV), God declares, "For I know the plans I have for you, declares the LORD to prosper you and not to harm you, plans to give you hope and a future." God wants His power to be manifested in your life. It's time to stop being led by your feelings! God wants you to be led by His Word. God's Word doesn't lie. God's Word doesn't have an expiration date. The truth of God's Word is forever settled in the heavens. The Scripture states in Matthew 24:35, "Heaven and earth shall pass away, but my words shall not pass away." You can stand firm upon God's Word.

God's Word will never change. God's Word will never diminish or lose its power. His Word will never return to Him void.

In Isaiah 55:11 (NKJV), God spoke these words, "So shall My word be that goes forth from My mouth; it shall not return to me void, but it shall accomplish what I please, and it shall prosper in the thing for which I sent it." When you begin to speak God's Word over your life, change will happen! The change might not occur immediately. However, be persistent to continually stand in faith. I am a witness. I love this cliche! "God may not come when you want Him, but He's always right on time!" Things will shift for you! There will be a visible display of God's hand at work in your life. Be determined not to give up or give in to the lies of the enemy. Keep your heart pure before God. Be relentless in your pursuit of wanting to know God in an intimate way. Pursue God with all your heart, soul, mind, and being. Spend time reading and being a doer of God's Word. Don't stop praying! Please don't you dare stop believing God! If the Spirit of God tells you to start a fast, then fast. When you pray in faith, you must not ask amiss or for selfish reasons, but keep your heart pure before God. Watch God Work! God wants to wow you with His goodness! God will deliver you! Dare to believe God to perform miracles for you.

Now, let's look at some people in the Bible who wouldn't take no for an answer. These pillars of faith believed God against all odds and impossibilities. Like these faith pioneers, God wants your faith to be so strong in Him that nothing will be able to shake it! You might say, "Is that possible?" You don't understand my struggle. I don't have to understand. I have complete confidence in the one true God in whom I serve. I know He is well able to deliver you! I know the power and authority He holds. I know He's able to do exceedingly above what we can ask or think. He's the creator of everything! Absolutely nothing is a match against His power!

Let's begin by looking at the lives of Abraham and Sarah. I love what Romans 4:18 states about Abraham. The Passion Translation reads, "Against all odds, when it looked hopeless, Abraham believed the promise and expected God to fulfill it." He took God at His Word, and as a result, he became the father of many nations. God's declaration over him came to pass: "Your descendants will be so many that they will be impossible to count!" Abraham expected God to fulfill the promise God gave to him. Where's your expectancy? Like Abraham, are you believing God to fulfill the promise(s)? The promise God made Abraham didn't happen immediately. It was approximately 25 years for this promise to manifest in Abraham's life. Most of us would have had the attitude of just forget it. "I'm tired of waiting. Oh, LORD, I can't wait any longer." No, Abraham had the posture of Lord, "I'm going to wait on you."

In our lives, we must mimic this same patience and perseverance. Abraham knew God made Him a promise. He didn't stop believing God because the promise didn't occur right away. I'm sure Abraham got frustrated and wanted to quit. The point is he didn't. In my mind, I can hear Abraham saying, "Lord, I gave up everything to follow you. The only thing missing in my life is the son You promised me. I began to believe you when I was 75. Now, God, I'm 99 years of age. The promise you made me has yet to happen for me." This didn't cause Abraham to doubt God. Abraham didn't quit and abandon the promise God had given to him. Consequently, Abraham guarded his promise from God and continued to have strong faith.

You might say, "Didn't Abraham try to take matters into his own hands?" The answer is yes, he did. At one point in the game, Sarah gave Abraham permission to impregnate her servant, Hagar. Clearly, Sarah got tired of waiting on God to make the promise of an heir happen. Therefore, Abraham obeyed his wife's command; as a result, her servant had a son by the name of Ishmael. This is found in Genesis 16. Later, we read that Sarah becomes jealous of her servant and there were consequences for taking matters into her own hands. When we try to rush God's timing and expedite His process, it will only create TROUBLE and heartache. God isn't obligated to bless things that we have orchestrated apart from Him. This truth is illustrated in Sarah and Abraham's experience. Sarah became jealous of Abraham's attention towards Ishmael and Hagar. The end result was Hagar and her son being banished from the camp. However, God did provide for Hagar and her son. Even though Sarah and Abraham acted impatiently, it did not thwart God's original promise. The promise of their own heir. I'm glad God is merciful towards us! He is a great Father. He still blesses us when we become impatient and deviate from His plans. Thank you, Jesus! The thing is when we refuse to wait on God by making it happen in our strength. We extend the waiting process. Also, we experience setbacks and turmoil that God didn't want us to face. I can testify from my own experiences, the hurt I endured from not allowing God to be God.

I can recall one time I purchased a car. I bought the first car I set my eyes upon based on me not wanting to wait on God's timing. That car was a hot mess! The engine ended up blowing up in this car, leaving me with nothing for a short period of time. From this experience, the next car I purchased, I waited for God to show me the right one to buy. I drove this car until it wouldn't run anymore. Recently, I just scrapped the car to a junkyard. When God is in the plan, you might have to go through hardship, but He will equip you and sustain you. He will provide every resource you need to help you become victorious. It's the waiting period that can cause us to be double-minded. James 1:8 reads, "A double minded man is unstable in all his ways." It's the waiting period that tries to steal our focus away from God's sovereignty. During times of waiting, we have to guard our minds. When frustration, weariness, and doubt tries to creep in, we have to renew our minds through God's word. I'm a witness that God will bless you when you learn to wait on Him. He will open doors no man can shut, He will bless you in unimaginable ways, and He will bless you with no strings attached.

Another way to guard your mind is to remember the ways God has delivered you in the past. Remind yourself of this fact. He did it before. He can do it again. I love what the Lord told Joshua to remind Israel when he was leading them out of the wilderness. In Joshua 4, God wanted Israel to build a memorial. We have to constantly remind ourselves of God's ability to perform the impossible. Keep a journal or notebook. Write down the miracles God has done for you. Revelation 12:11 mentions how we overcome by the blood of the lamb and the word of our testimony. Don't be ashamed to tell your testimony! Shout it everywhere you go, the marvelous things God has done for you and those around you. This is how we stir and keep our faith charged. Stay around people who are faith builders, not faith drainers. Faith drainers are the ones who try to tell you why things can't and won't happen for you. Ask God to give you a deaf ear to people who are faith drainers. Pray and ask God to send people of faith to you. These will be people who will encourage you to believe God when the odds seem like it will never happen.

Thirdly, have a posture of worship as you wait for God's timing. God doesn't want us waiting in doubt, unbelief, and complaining. 1 Thessalonians 5:18 says, "In everything give thanks; for this is the will of God in Christ Jesus concerning you." God wants us to have a grateful heart. I'm not sure where this quote was derived. It's true and very fitting for this chapter. The quote is, "You praise, you'll be raised! You doubt, you'll go without! You complain, you'll remain. Worship lifts us higher!"

You might ask, "How does it lift me higher?" Worship lifts us into God's presence. When we worship God, it gets His attention. God desires our worship and He wants us to give Him our full devotion. Psalm 37:4 says, "Delight yourself in the LORD, and he will give you the desires of your heart." Delight defined by Webster's 1828 dictionary is a high degree of pleasure, or satisfaction of mind; joy. We should take great joy and pleasure in spending time with our Heavenly Father. We owe Him our time, our mind (attention), our bodies, or to simply put it... our everything. When we learn to take satisfaction in Him, then His blessings will flow freely. Why? We chose to worship the Creator over the creation. We chose to put Him first. God loves it when we dote over Him. He loves to hear our voices sing praises to Him. He loves for us to tell Him how much we need Him. When we put God first, it ensures God that we won't forget Him when He gives us the desires of our hearts. God always wants to be number one in our lives.

Like any good parent, there is nothing God won't do for His children to demonstrate His love. Matthew 7:11 says, "If you then, who are evil, know how to give good gifts to your children, how much more will your Father who is heaven give good things to those who ask Him!" God wants to bless you! Again, we must love HIM wholeheartedly and keep HIM number one. Abraham applied this principle in his life. At the ripe age of 100 years old, God honored His promise. He blessed Abraham and Sarah with a son. When God blesses you with the promise you desired most from Him, continue to worship the Blesser and not the blessing. Abraham was willing to sacrifice his son out of his loyalty and devotion to God. Consequently, God provided a ram in the thicket for Abraham to sacrifice. God requires loyalty and complete devotion to Him.

Lastly, we must look at Hannah's life. We find the life of Hannah in 1 Samuel 1. Hannah is one of the wives of Elkanah. Elkanah's other wife is Peninnah. You see, the Lord had shut up Hannah's womb. Hannah was barren and was desperate to have a baby. Are you desperate for God to move in your life? Be patient. Wait on God's timing! Be encouraged! God will perform the impossible for you! Back to Hannah, year after year, she couldn't conceive a child. This caused Hannah much grief. Peninnah was the other wife of Elkanah. She had several children by Elkanah. This caused Hannah to develop deep sadness and despair within her heart. Peninnah knew this bothered Hannah, so she would taunt Hannah and make fun of her because she couldn't bear a child. Regardless of Hannah's bareness, she was deeply loved by her husband. God deeply loves you. Don't allow other people's insecurity to make you feel less than how God sees you. Please do yourself a favor and block out the noise of your Peninah's. This illustrates to me how the enemy loves to taunt us. He will use people to distract you from your purpose. Stay focused on God's promise. No matter what the enemy throws at you, please keep your eyes on Jesus.

Beloved, don't listen to the voice of your critics. Stay in prayer! Stay the course and let no one distract you. You are a chosen vessel of God. God has a great destiny waiting for you! You have been destined by God to win!!! Can you imagine how Hannah felt? She probably felt so much anguish and contempt due to her bareness. I can attest in my life of how it feels to be waiting half your life for God's promises to come to pass. I understand rejection quite well. Also, I understand how it feels to think God has forgotten you and to be overlooked by man. Beloved, as God's mouthpiece, I want to proclaim, "God has not forgotten you." God sent me, yes, little ole me, Terra Dobson, to remind you that He is going to bless you and He rewards those who diligently seeks Him. God isn't finished writing our story. There is a divine plan for you and me that our Father is manifesting within the earth.

At the age of forty-five, I'm just now seeing God's plan for my life begin to unfold. Age is nothing for God. He is the time keeper! I'm excited about this new thing He's doing in my life. Let's keep it real and allow me to be transparent. Did I want to quit? Yes. Did I want to give up and throw in the towel? The answer is yes! The one thing I know is God is a keeper. God continues to be faithful in my life and He keeps me in perfect peace. I decree by faith, God is doing a new thing in your life. God is going to blow your mind! Get ready for the breakthroughs! The people who ridiculed you and laughed at you will have to eat their negative words against you! God is giving you elevation and causing you to be victorious in every barren place in your life.

We must follow Hannah's example of faith. As Hannah prayed and believed God against all odds, we too must stand in faith. At the appointed time, the LORD blessed Hannah with a son. Hannah's son would be named Samuel. He became a prophet and judge for Israel. After the birth of Samuel, God blessed Hannah with five other children.

God will use every part of your life for His glory. He will use the wasted years, failures, and your mistakes. The only thing you have to do is stay in faith! Keep believing God for the impossible. Watch God work! He is going to blow your mind and silence the voice of your critics and the naysayers. You're coming out! This is your year for God to perform the impossible for you! I want to end with Philippians 1:6, "Being confident of this very thing, that he which hath begun a good work in you will perform it until the day of Jesus Christ."

My Testimony

I took God at His word and now my life is changing! Wow, is all I can say... I am in awe of God's goodness in my life. I never thought in a million years that I would start blogging and become an author of a book. It's not because I'm a prolific writer or a Biblical scholar, but it's only by the goodness and grace of God. I want to challenge you if I can do it, you can too. Don't worry about punctuation or grammatical errors that is the editor's job. All you have to do is write!

Prayer

Heavenly Father, thank You for loving us. Thank You for keeping us! Lord, I ask You to bless the person who is reading this prayer. Lord, I ask You to allow them to feel Your presence in a tangible way. Lord, meet all their needs according to Your riches in glory through Christ Jesus. Encourage them. Heavenly Father, let them know that you haven't forgotten them! Help them to believe You beyond what they can see with their natural eyes! Stir up their faith and allow them to see that You are working on their behalf. What the enemy meant for bad, turn it around for their good and Your glory, Lord. Let them know all things are working together for their good. Allow them to see the vision You have ordained for their lives. Do the impossible for them and through them! Use them for your glory! In the name of Jesus. Amen.

About The Author

On February 25, 2017, Terra became a licensed and ordained minister. Terra began ministry at the age of 23. After a series of dreams and verbal confirmations, she announced her call into ministry in 1997. In the dreams God gave her, she would always see herself preaching, prophesying, laying hands, and praying for people. God would always give her the Scripture to read in Jeremiah 1:5. After the Holy Spirit gave Terra the revelation of her dreams, she knew that God had called her to be a prophet. She preached her first sermon at the church her grandfather founded.

Terra's other Kingdom assignments include G.L.O.W. (God's Love Overflowing Within). She originally founded this ministry in July 2017 but didn't launch it until May 2020. The purpose of this ministry is to equip, empower, and encourage female ministers. Also, to encourage women in general. Under GLOW ministries, Terra host women's empowerment luncheons. Terra is a prophetic voice in the body of Christ. She is also an avid student and teacher of God's word. Terra is passionate about preaching the Word of God!

The thing most important about her is that she loves the LORD and His people. She loves spending time with God in prayer and worship. She has the heart of an intercessor. She loves serving and praying for others. She desires to see the body of Christ walking in maturity and helping other believers in Christ to reach their God-given potential.

Index

A

abide, 29
Abraham, 4, 5, 85, 86, 87, 88, 92
abundantly, 2
abuse, 48
accomplish, 1, 9, 22, 45, 84
accountability, 11, 14
accurately, 62
addiction, 13
adores, 43
advantage, 48
affection, 38
afraid, 10, 14, 31, 46, 58, 60, 63, 66, 67, 73

alarm, 62, 66
alignment, 8, 33
Almighty, 20
ambitions, 40
ambushes, 50
angel, 9
angry, 31, 37, 52, 63
annihilate, 43
anoint, 31
ant, 9
Apple Store, 5
ashamed, 11, 89
assassinate, 2
assignment, 1, 7, 18, 22, 27, 30, 32
attention, 26, 27, 87, 90, 91
attitude, 13, 86
authority, 4, 29, 32, 61, 63, 64, 65, 71, 85
avoidance, 2

B

background, 57
bad habit, 13
bareness, 93
battles, 50, 70

believe, 7, 8, 22, 23, 28, 29, 39, 42, 50, 54, 61, 62, 65, 68, 69, 70, 71, 75, 78, 79, 81, 82, 85, 86, 90, 97
betrayed, 48
Bible, 9, 19, 28, 85
bidding, 2
blessings, 9, 31, 33, 91
block, 51, 61, 69, 93
blood, 50, 64, 66, 71, 89
blueprint, 5, 6, 25
BOLD, 66
boldly, 4, 39
book, 3, 15, 20, 25, 40, 42, 45, 53, 54, 67, 96
Book of the Law, 82
boundaries, 48, 60
brave, 1, 18
breakthroughs, 94

C

captivity, 78
cares, 2, 60, 65
catapult, 42
chains, 60
characteristics, 12
cheated, 4, 40

Cheer, 46
cheerleader, 4, 44
choice, 57
choices, 7, 10
Christ, 3, 6, 8, 12, 13, 15, 22, 37, 38, 49, 56, 61, 63, 71, 90, 95, 96, 99
Christian, 39
churches, 22
circumstances, 75, 82
clay, 24
comfort zone, 30
committee, 14
complain, 90
complete, 3, 10, 59, 64, 65, 85, 92
confidence, 28, 59, 85
confident, 3, 28, 30, 95
confusion, 3, 5, 36
connection, 34, 35, 36, 40, 51, 54
Connection, 34
conquer, 72
consecrate, 50
consistent, 10, 11, 30
contradict, 29
control, 26, 62, 63, 66
convince, 3, 4, 5
courageous, 26, 57, 66, 73

created, 2, 8, 19, 21, 22, 23, 31, 55, 57, 59, 60, 66
creativity, 61
Creator, 18, 19, 33, 44, 59, 91
creature, 59
credibility, 28
cross, 48, 65

D

darkness, 50, 59, 77
dead, 2, 8, 64
deadline, 2
death, 43, 45, 57
decision, 57, 67, 69
decision maker, 57
declaration, 22, 62, 71, 86
Declare, 1, 8, 15, 49, 52
deeper, 12, 62, 78
defeat, 6, 70
delay, 1, 76
delays, 14
Delight, 91
deliverance, 77
deliverer, 27, 67
demeanor, 60, 76
demonic spirit, 62, 64

demons, 29
denials, 14
derail, 2, 61, 93
descendants, 86
deserve, 48
desires, 32, 40, 90, 91, 99
despair, 78, 92
destiny, 2, 18, 42, 51, 52, 53, 57, 61, 64, 70, 93
destroy, 2
destroyer, 52
determined, 2, 5, 7, 38, 63, 84
development, 54
devil, 63
devotion, 38, 91, 92
diligently, 22, 94
disappointed, 52
discern, 55
discernment, 12, 53
discouraged, 46, 66
discrimination, 24
diseases, 29
disobedience, 31
disobedient, 27
divine, 24, 38, 51, 77, 94
DNA, 15, 66
doors, 33, 40, 57, 77, 89

doubt, 3, 23, 29, 40, 67, 73, 76, 79, 86, 89, 90
dread,, 62
dreams, 98

E

ears, 36, 58, 79
earth, 1, 2, 18, 19, 30, 59, 65, 69, 83, 94
effective, 2, 9, 14, 20, 30, 50
elevated, 66, 81
elevation, 40, 41, 80, 94
Elohim, 19
eloquent speaker, 30, 60
emotional hype, 79
emotions, 35, 69, 70, 81
Empower, 73
encourage, 4, 11, 13, 20, 43, 52, 54, 61, 65, 76, 83, 90, 99
enemies, 42, 44, 45, 50
enemy, 2, 3, 32, 39, 44, 47, 50, 61, 63, 64, 65, 70, 71, 76, 77, 84, 93, 97
equip, 64, 88, 99
escape, 37, 69, 76
establish, 38, 49
Esther, 42, 43, 44, 45
evil, 44, 45, 91

excuse, 17, 18, 20, 25, 27, 28, 29, 30, 31
Excuses, 17, 21
execute, 24

F

fail, 22, 31, 43, 47
failures, 95
faith, 4, 7, 8, 15, 22, 29, 31, 43, 44, 65, 67, 68, 71, 77, 79, 80, 81, 82, 84, 85, 87, 90, 94, 95, 97
faith drainers, 90
Faith drainers, 90
faithful, 13, 83, 94
faithfulness, 50, 54, 69, 77
False Evidence Appearing Real, 67
false perception, 6
false perceptions, 21
familiar, 58
famous, 39
fasting, 50
Father, 6, 14, 15, 20, 23, 24, 33, 35, 38, 39, 40, 41, 46, 48, 58, 65, 67, 73, 78, 80, 88, 91, 94, 96
favorable, 81
fear, 22, 26, 27, 58, 61, 62, 63, 64, 65, 66, 67, 68, 72, 73
fearless, 23

fellowship, 55
female ministers, 99
fighting, 42, 44, 68, 76
fire, 26, 30
flesh, 19, 50, 78
focus, 21, 22, 27, 40, 65, 71, 89
foolish, 28, 41
foot stools, 42
forsake, 46, 68
forsaken, 76
forward, 26, 32, 52, 56, 80
freedom, 9, 64, 65, 68, 73
Freedom, 64
friend, 18, 25, 27, 31, 45, 46, 59, 66
fright, 62
fruit, 36, 82
frustrated, 37, 86
fulfill, 4, 17, 85, 86
future, 83

G

gemstone, 65
Genesis, 4, 19, 45, 87
gifts, 21, 41, 54, 91
glass ceiling, 61

glory, 1, 8, 40, 55, 56, 59, 66, 95, 96, 97
goal, 2
goals, 10
God, 1, 2, 3, 4, 5, 6, 7, 8, 9, 10, 11, 12, 13, 14, 15, 17, 18, 19, 20, 21, 22, 23, 24, 25, 26, 27, 28, 29, 30, 31, 32, 33, 34, 35, 36, 37, 38, 39, 40, 41, 42, 43, 44, 45, 46, 47, 48, 49, 50, 51, 52, 53, 54, 55, 57, 58, 59, 60, 61, 62, 63, 64, 65, 66, 67, 68, 69, 70, 71, 72, 73, 75, 76, 77, 78, 79, 80, 81, 82, 83, 84, 85, 86, 87, 88, 89, 90, 91, 92, 93, 94, 95, 96, 98, 99
good, 11, 13, 30, 41, 45, 46, 47, 53, 55, 58, 71, 75, 76, 91, 95, 97
goodness, 31, 54, 77, 85, 96
gossip, 13
grammatical errors, 96
grateful, 24, 39, 53, 54, 72, 90
greatness, 15, 27, 42, 51, 54
guard, 47, 58, 70, 89

H

Hagar, 87
Hannah, 92, 93, 94, 95
happy, 10, 12, 50, 66
harm, 45, 83

harvest, 10, 11, 20
Health, 80
hearing, 4, 80, 82
heart, 3, 6, 12, 24, 32, 46, 57, 61, 62, 69, 70, 75, 76, 84, 90, 91, 93, 99
heartbreak, 46
hearts, 18, 26, 38, 47, 79, 91
heavenly realm, 7
heavens, 19, 83
heir, 87, 88
helmet of salvation, 70
help, 10, 11, 12, 13, 14, 16, 20, 23, 30, 40, 47, 52, 53, 54, 55, 63, 73, 78, 88
Helper, 6
hesitation, 32
Hewlett Packard, 5
hidden, 56, 57
Holy Spirit, 4, 6, 10, 16, 17, 25, 26, 27, 29, 35, 36, 37, 38, 40, 47, 48, 49, 52, 53, 55, 57, 58, 60, 63, 64, 73, 98
honor, 40, 55, 83
hope, 6, 21, 25, 58, 72, 83
hopeless, 8, 77, 78, 85
hopelessness, 78
house, 6
humble, 24

hurt, 46, 47, 49, 64, 88

I

ideas, 1, 3
identify, 12, 35, 37, 52
identity, 3, 36
idolatry, 21
illumination, 52
impatient, 88
impossibilities, 81, 85
impossible, 22, 40, 61, 64, 69, 79, 85, 86, 89, 92, 95, 97
inadequacies, 27
inadequate, 21, 32
ineffective, 14, 62
infallible Word, 74
infirmities, 12
influence, 34
influencer, 57
inheritance, 64
inner circle, 47, 48
insecurity, 93
instruction, 29, 80
instructions, 8, 27, 28, 29, 78, 79
insults, 79

iron, 53, 54
Ishmael, 87
Israel, 27, 37, 45, 66, 78, 89, 95
Israelites, 57

J

jealous, 87
jealousy, 14
Jeremiah, 19, 21, 23, 24, 25, 78, 83, 98
Jesus, 2, 9, 16, 22, 29, 33, 35, 36, 40, 41, 47, 48, 49, 52, 55, 61, 63, 64, 65, 66, 68, 71, 72, 73, 74, 88, 90, 93, 95, 96, 97
job, 17, 31, 59, 62, 67, 96
joke, 60
Joshua, 26, 57, 58, 66, 82, 89
journal, 89
journey, 12, 18, 58, 68
Joy, 80
Judas, 47
judge, 39, 53, 95
judgmental, 14

K

kill, 2, 39, 43, 64

Kingdom, 3, 36, 99
kingship, 79

L

launch, 42, 58, 73, 99
leader, 30, 54, 57, 66
leading, 20, 24, 37, 89
leprous, 29
level, 13, 46
liberty, 68, 73
lies, 3, 32, 39, 71, 77, 84
life, 2, 3, 4, 5, 6, 7, 9, 10, 13, 14, 18, 21, 22, 24, 25, 26, 31, 32, 35, 37, 39, 41, 43, 44, 45, 47, 49, 51, 52, 53, 60, 61, 63, 64, 65, 66, 67, 68, 69, 72, 73, 75, 76, 77, 78, 79, 80, 81, 83, 84, 86, 92, 93, 94, 95, 96
lifeless, 64
limbo, 3, 5
limitations, 21, 27, 60, 79, 81
logically, 71
LORD, 6, 9, 11, 16, 18, 19, 20, 21, 23, 24, 25, 26, 28, 31, 32, 36, 37, 45, 49, 51, 55, 58, 66, 67, 69, 70, 73, 78, 80, 82, 83, 86, 91, 95, 99

love, 13, 14, 20, 24, 25, 27, 30, 36, 38, 40, 43, 45, 46, 48, 49, 53, 54, 60, 62, 64, 65, 67, 70, 80, 84, 85, 89, 91, 92
LOVE, 64
loyalty, 92

M

MacBook Air, 5
main stage, 8
masterpiece, 21
maturity, 99
measure, 78
mediocrity, 7, 21
meditate, 70, 82
mentality, 12
mentored, 57
Merriam Webster dictionary, 63
mighty, 42
mind, 2, 3, 6, 8, 50, 61, 62, 69, 70, 71, 72, 77, 78, 83, 84, 86, 89, 91, 94, 95
minds, 5, 37, 40, 69, 70, 73, 74, 89
mindset, 22, 75
ministry, 21, 23, 38, 47, 54, 98, 99
miracles, 29, 89
mistake, 31

money, 6, 17
Mordecai, 42, 43, 44, 45, 50
Moses, 26, 27, 28, 29, 30, 31, 54, 57
mountain, 5, 37
mouth, 24, 25, 26, 30, 61, 65, 82, 84
muzzle, 61, 65

N

nations, 23, 85
natural eyes, 69, 82, 97
naysayers, 42, 44, 81, 95
negative thoughts, 22, 32, 33, 44, 70
negativity, 14
nervous, 27
news, 41, 45, 46, 64, 66, 71
notebook, 89

O

obedience, 31, 57, 68
obey, 4, 5, 8, 20, 68, 79, 80
obscurity, 42
opinions, 37, 44, 60
opportunity, 24, 41
ordained, 10, 18, 22, 26, 35, 46, 55, 80, 97, 98

overcome, 2, 6, 13, 16, 58, 64, 89
Overcoming, 56
overlooked, 40, 57, 93
overnight, 58

P

paralyze, 26, 32, 61
paths, 6
peace, 24, 44, 48, 72, 94
Peace, 80
Peninnah, 92, 93
perfect peace, 72
personal, 3, 11, 20, 43, 54, 67
personality, 21, 27, 31, 59
phobia, 62
Phobos, 62
plans, 4, 9, 45, 83, 88
pleasure, 91
pleasures, 39
potential, 9, 16, 53, 99
potter, 24
power, 2, 17, 20, 25, 27, 29, 30, 31, 35, 43, 44, 51, 61, 62, 63, 64, 67, 69, 77, 83, 84, 85
powerful, 19, 53, 58, 62, 63, 82
prayer, 6, 46, 47, 50, 52, 73, 93, 96, 99

preaching, 27, 28, 54, 98, 99
presence, 37, 67, 72, 90, 96
pride, 14
principalities, 50
process, 29, 57, 58, 73, 87, 88
procrastination, 2, 5, 6, 8, 9, 10, 14, 15, 16
promise keeper, 77
promised, 1, 72, 86
Promised Land', 19
promises, 8, 69, 76, 79, 80, 81, 82, 93
promotion, 38, 39, 40, 41, 42
promptings, 20, 24
prophesy, 32, 37, 53
prophet, 23, 95, 98
prophetic word, 32
Prophets, 54
prosper, 51, 82, 83, 84
public speaker, 30
punctuation, 96
purpose, 2, 3, 4, 7, 13, 17, 18, 19, 26, 33, 34, 35, 36, 37, 38, 45, 51, 53, 59, 61, 62, 66, 77, 93, 99

Q

qualified, 19
quarrel, 39

question, 3, 23, 80
quote, 22, 23, 90

R

rebellion, 26
rejection, 93
relationship, 12, 13, 20, 34, 35, 38, 48, 78
reliance, 35
remembrance, 6, 32
renegade, 47
repetitive cycle, 79
respecter, 43, 67
restoration, 25, 83
revelation, 12, 18, 35, 37, 38, 62, 65, 98
reward, 11, 47
rewards, 31, 68, 94
riches, 96
righteousness, 38
root, 61

S

sacrifice, 92
sadness, 77, 92
safe, 65

safety nets, 57
Sarah, 85, 87, 92
satisfaction, 91
Saul, 79
scholar, 60, 96
scorpions, 64
Scripture, 2, 3, 8, 9, 20, 22, 23, 25, 28, 31, 45, 61, 62, 69, 70, 77, 78, 82, 83, 98
seat of the scornful, 70
secret, 25, 51
seeking, 5, 37, 38, 48, 78
Selah, 44, 59
self-esteem, 33
self-image, 33
selfish, 40, 84
serpents, 64
servant, 87
setbacks, 14, 88
shame, 28, 42, 83
shift, 69, 80, 84
shock, 21
shortcomings, 48
sing, 60, 91
sins, 13
situation, 8, 81
situations, 2

sluggard, 9, 10
snake, 29
sovereignty, 78, 89
speech impediment, 30
Spirit of God, 17, 36, 57, 60, 84
spiritual, 19, 43, 50, 54
spiritual crutches, 19
spiritual wickedness, 50
spiritually blind, 63
spotlight, 8, 40
springboard, 42
stability, 81
status quo, 4, 66
steadfast, 52
strength, 8, 17, 20, 22, 25, 27, 63, 88
strengthens, 3
strengths, 31
stronghold, 19
stuck, 2, 3, 4, 5, 8, 32, 35, 37, 54, 63, 68, 79
student, 99
succeed, 11, 82
success, 2
suffers, 13
sufficiency, 28
supernatural, 77
supportive, 53

sure word, 28
survive, 13
sustain, 31, 88
sword, 64

T

table, 57
teach, 6, 25, 40, 47
teachable, 24
teaching, 28, 54, 73
tears, 77
temptation, 77
territory, 58
terror, 62
Testimony, 15, 32, 96
thief, 2
thrive, 13
time, 1, 2, 3, 4, 5, 6, 7, 8, 9, 11, 14, 16, 17, 18, 19, 26, 29, 31, 35, 36, 37, 41, 42, 46, 52, 56, 57, 58, 60, 62, 63, 65, 68, 77, 78, 79, 80, 83, 84, 88, 91, 94, 95, 99
timidity, 27
tongue, 30
top dog, 41
torment, 65

tortured, 60
trap, 11
tricks, 2
triumph, 68
trouble, 9, 53
trust worthy, 24
truth, 4, 12, 13, 26, 33, 37, 52, 80, 83, 87
turmoil, 88
tyranny, 27

U

unbelief, 73, 79, 90
undefeated, 44
underdog, 22, 41, 42, 80
understand, 5, 58, 62, 85, 93
understanding, 6
unimaginable, 89
unrighteousness, 13
unstable, 81, 89
unstoppable, 75
unworthy, 57
upgrade, 41
urgency, 7

V

validation, 5, 29
value, 3, 65
Vengeance, 50
victories, 44
victorious, 9, 15, 33, 65, 88, 94
victory, 9, 65, 68
videos, 73
viewpoint, 24, 60
vindicator, 68
vision, 5, 11, 21, 51, 76, 97
voice, 18, 26, 30, 35, 36, 57, 59, 77, 80, 93, 95, 99

W

warfare, 50
warning, 52
water, 9, 82
weaknesses, 31
weary, 11
window, 24, 27
winds of change, 57
wings of faith, 80
winner, 15
wisdom, 12, 26, 47, 49, 53
wise, 9, 28, 42, 58

wisely, 9, 16
witness, 20, 32, 68, 77, 84, 89, 93
womb, 21, 92
women, 53, 54, 99
word curse, 51
word curses, 42, 49, 51
Word of God, 29, 64, 99
worship, 50, 90, 91, 92, 99
worthy, 31, 46, 69
write, 3, 15, 53, 54, 60, 96
writing, 15, 40, 62, 79, 94